Carol Joyce has been a professional textile designer for many years. She presently teaches a textile design course that she introduced at the School of Visual Arts in New York in 1965.

Designing for printed textiles

a guide to studio and free-lance work

Carol Joyce

A SPECTRUM BOOK   PRENTICE-HALL, INC.   Englewood Cliffs, N.J. 07632

Library of Congress Cataloging in Publication Data

Joyce, Carol.
   Designing for printed textiles.

  "A Spectrum Book."
  Bibliography: p.
  Includes index.
  1. Textile design. 2. Textile printing. I. Title.
NK9500.J65   746.6   81-17776
                    AACR2

ISBN 0-13-201319-3 {PBK}

ISBN 0-13-201327-4

This Spectrum Book is available to businesses and organizations at a special discount when ordered in large quantities. For information, contact Prentice-Hall, Inc., General Publishing Division, Special Sales, Englewood Cliffs, N.J. 07632.

Editorial production/supervision and interior design by Cyndy Lyle Rymer
Page layout by Diane Heckler-Kohromas
Manufacturing buyer: Cathie Lenard
Interior illustrations by Carol Joyce
Cover design by Jeannette Jacobs
Individual cover panels by (left to right) Jack Lenor Larsen, © 1967;
Brunshwig & Fils, Inc.; Carol Joyce
Within the color insert, Color Plate 12, *Pomegranate*, 1973 © Jack Lenor Larsen, Inc.; Color Plate 13, *Bukhara*, 1972 © Jack Lenor Larsen, Inc.

Prentice-Hall International, Inc., *London*
Prentice-Hall of Australia Pty. Limited, *Sydney*
Prentice-Hall of Canada, Ltd., *Toronto*
Prentice-Hall of India Private Limited, *New Delhi*
Prentice-Hall of Japan, Inc., *Tokyo*
Prentice-Hall of Southeast Asia Pte. Ltd., *Singapore*
Whitehall Books Limited, *Wellington, New Zealand*

Contents

Preface

A textile design begins as an idea on paper and ends printed on cloth. Happily, it serves both a useful and an esthetic function. The designer's job is to combine her or his skills, taste, and imagination to produce good designs, and that's what this book is all about. It is a complete course in the creation of designs to be commercially printed on fabric, and it covers all aspects of studio and free-lance work.

The history of printed textile design is a long and fascinating one. As early as 3000 B.C. patterned cloth was widely used by primitive people. A thousand years later in Egypt and Peru, clothing decorated with stamped patterns was being worn. Examples of printed cloth from Greece survive from the fourth and fifth centuries A.D., and evidence exists that printed cotton was in use at Benin, Nigeria, by the thirteenth century.

Europeans wore printed fabrics as early as 1100. And in 1712 George Leason set up the first American cotton-printing works in Boston. More than a billion yards of printed fabric are produced in the United States every year. The textile apparel industry ranks second in the country in terms of employment. It is hard to estimate how many designs are used in the printing of billions of yards of goods, but it is a great many, you can be sure.

For many years I have been a designer, and since 1965, the textile design instructor at The School of Visual Arts in New York City. I have received numerous inquiries from students, teachers, and other designers seeking a text describing the various steps in the creation and preparation of textile designs. This book was written to fill that need.

It is a learning aid for textile design classes and a home study guide for those desiring to learn on their own. It will also prove valuable to professionals in allied fields, such as fashion and interior design, and to artists and crafts people who wish to broaden their commercial skills.

Acknowledgments

I would like to especially thank my husband, Bob Joyce, to whom this book is dedicated, and my mother-in-law, Margaret Joyce, for their expert editing and moral support throughout this project.

I also want to express my appreciation to Ruth Soffer, Joan Nelsen, and Frank Delfino for their artistic contributions, and to Maggie Soffer for her general help.

For their generous assistance and time, thanks to Leon Hecht, Lynn Johnson, Lou Horowitz, Jonathan Katz, Shirley Davidson, Glenda White, Janice Brown, Gregory Baron, Sandy Lustig, Sidney Zweibel, Yves Mahé, Jeffrey S. Byer, Geeta Manansingh, Melanie Pinto, Susan S. Freedman, Robert Burger, Thomas F. Lee, Ogden Starr, O. J. Stewart-Liberty, Mary B. Galpin, Inez Negroñ Peña, James M. Donovan, Jr., Anka Lefebvre, Pierre LeVec, Ola Pfeifer, Devorah Buxbaum, Leslie Warren, Sigmon Huitt, and Peter Gefken.

Special thanks to Glyn P. Cloyd, who photographed all the textile designs and fabrics in the book, and to Shirley Sulat for her expert typing.

The following companies were most cooperative in helping me gather material for the book: Bloomcraft Fabrics, Inc.; Boussac of France, Inc.; Brunschwig & Fils, Inc.; Burlington Industries; China Seas, Inc.; Clarence House Imports, Ltd.; The Cloth Company, Division of Cranston Print Works Co.; First Editions, Inc.; Jack Lenor Larsen, Inc.; Liberty of London, Inc.; Martex, Division of Westpoint Pepperell; Schwartz Liebman Textiles; F. Schumacher and Co.; Souleiado Collection at Pierre Deux; Springs Mills, Inc.; Sublistatic Corporation of America; American Textile Manufacturers Institute, Inc.; and Museum Books, Inc.

Chapter one

Introduction to textile design

Apparel and home furnishing

There are two broad categories of printed fabric designs: apparel and home furnishing.

Apparel designs are for any type of fabric that is meant to be worn — women's wear (blouse, dress, swimwear, lingerie, etc.), men's wear, and children's clothing.

Home-furnishing designs are for any fabric that is used in the home or elsewhere for interior decoration. They include drapery, upholstery, wallpaper, and so on (known as decoratives), and sheets and pillowcases, towels and bedspreads, and the like (known as domestics).

Responsibilities of the designer

The three skills a textile designer must develop are designing, coloring, and doing repeats. An individual may specialize in any one of these skills but should master all of them, as all are required in most studios and other jobs.

1

DESIGNING

A textile design starts with an idea or a theme. The designer then selects the appropriate reference material for developing the idea, combining it with creative imagination, layout, and color sense to create the design (see Chapter 5).

COLORING

The selection of colors for a design is very important. A commonplace design can be greatly improved by good color. Conversely, a really good design can be ruined by bad color (see Chapter 6).

A set of three or more color combinations is created and printed along with each pattern. These sets are called colorings, color combinations, or colorways.

REPEATS

A repeat is the final version of a design, worked out and painted to meet the exact specifications of the printing process. (See Chapter 7 for complete instructions for making repeats.)

Converters

There are two main sources of jobs for textile designers: converters and design studios. A converter is a company that converts unprinted fabric, called *gray goods*, into printed fabric. The converter takes care of all the processes, from purchasing the gray goods to shipping the printed goods to the clothing manufacturers.

Most converters have one or more studios that employ designers, colorists, and repeat artists. The large apparel converters often have separate studios for dress wear, men's wear, swimwear, and so on. The large home furnishing converters have separate studios for domestics and decoratives. The largest converting houses have both apparel and home furnishing studios, and therefore maintain a staff of textile artists. Small converters may have only one or two designers.

A converting job is salaried, and the company owns everything you do during working hours. In the busy seasons, there is often the opportunity to free lance for the company. This work is either done at home or overtime at the studio. The arrangement for payment can be on an hourly basis or for a fee based on the current free-lance rates. The company usually has its own policy for payment, and it is wise to find it out before doing the work.

A job with a converter could include design, color combinations, and repeats, although some places hire separate colorists or repeat artists. When being interviewed for a job, always be sure what your responsibilities will be.

There are some benefits from working on a salary that are not available in free-lance work. Most companies have medical and insurance plans and give paid vacations and sick days. They also offer the possibility of moving into a better position. One of the opportunities they present for a higher job category is going to the mill and learning how to take charge of printing the patterns. You will be accompanied to the mill by an experienced person until you can handle the strike-offs by yourself. The strike-offs are the first run of yardage that is printed on a pattern. The printing and color on the fabric must be checked for accuracy. Corrections must be made immediately or the pattern pulled or stopped until further discussion with the stylist can be had.

The stylist

The stylist is the person in each studio who selects the designs to be printed in each line. Therefore, that person "styles the line." At a converter, the stylist is the one who hands out the work, directs the studio, and is responsible to company executives. In a design studio there is usually one person who is in overall charge and acts in the capacity of stylist.

The stylist goes to the mill to do the strike-offs or trains an assistant to do it and makes the final decisions on the patterns. The assistant stylist takes over in the studio when the stylist is out of town or otherwise unavailable.

Design studios

A design studio usually operates on a work-space arrangement. When you work on a free-lance basis, the studio acts as your agent and you get paid only for designs that are sold. The studio supplies a desk, salespersons, and direction concerning the types of designs its customers require. The designer must try to be disciplined about keeping regular hours, mutually agreed on, and should work at a reasonably steady pace. This assures the designer of the best chance for sales, since the studio will have a continued interest in the artistic development and sales of a reliable designer.

Either the salesperson takes the design collection to the

customers or the latter come to the studio to look for purchases. When a design is sold and delivered, the studio bills the customer. There is a standard price for designs, color combinations, and repeats. The studio takes a commission on every piece of work it sells. For many decades the standard commission has been 30 to 40 percent.

A design can be sold as a sketch or in repeat. The designer usually puts his or her own design into repeat, although a repeat artist provided by the studio may be used, payment for the repeat coming out of the designer's share of the money. The designer owns all the designs made at the studio, and these can be taken out at a prearranged time to make up a portfolio to use in job hunting.

Free-lance sales can be good one week and non-existent the next. Because of this inconsistency, free-lance work must be given time to develop, and progress should be evaluated on a quarterly or semiannual basis. This presents psychological as well as financial problems. A designer must be patient and must have some other source of income while developing a steady rate of sales.

The studio often provides special-order work for which payment is assured, which is of some financial help. It is also permissible to work on your own time for other contacts if there is no conflict of interest. Work should not be done for a rival studio or for one that does very similar styling. You can accept work from a studio that designs for apparel if your studio designs for home furnishings, or you can take outside work for women's wear if your studio designs for men's wear, and so on.

Many converters make it very clear that your job is in jeopardy if you work for anyone else. They fear the disclosure and copying of their line before they themselves can put it on the market. Some design studios also take this attitude, so it is wise to develop and follow a code of ethics that is workable for you and acceptable to your employer.

Some designers use a studio as their agent but work at home. The same discipline is required at home as in a studio if sales potential is to be developed. For instance, the head of the studio may make an arrangement for you to deliver your designs on Monday and at the same time give you directions for the following week's work. This insures your maintaining a steady work pace and constant contact with the studio. The payment and commission are the same for those who work in the studio as for those who work at home. It is a good idea to keep a record book of designs sold and other work done. Each piece will have a number and should be dated for delivery and payment. You will need these records also for your income tax.

It is also possible in some design studios to get a salaried job or to make other financial arrangements, such as commissions on sales plus some salary.

Agents

There are a number of individuals who will act as your agent to sell your designs for a commission but do not have work space to offer you. They have only offices or showrooms. In an arrangement with such an agent, you work at home and the agent gives you directions for designs, sells the designs, bills the customers, and pays you after collecting the amount due. These agents usually charge the same commission as the design studios, but it is well to make certain of the percentage they will take and the length of time it will take them to pay you after the delivery of the finished work. (These are the two things I hear the most complaints about from students.) I also recommend that you check with someone in the field or The Textile Designers Guild (see Bibliography for information) to make sure the agent you are considering is reputable and not a fly-by-night operator who will leave you with the problems of collecting payments and/or getting your designs back.

Free-lance: acting as your own agent

It is possible, of course, to act as your own agent, selling your designs and doing free-lance color combinations and repeats. However, this is difficult to do until you are established and have contacts who know your work and have confidence in you. The big advantage in acting as your own agent is, naturally, that you eliminate the agent's commission on sales while charging the same price the agent would. The disadvantage is having to deal with the problems that arise with customers, such as arbitrary changes in the work, disagreements about instructions, picking up and delivering work (perhaps several times if changes are being made), making new contacts, and collecting payments. All this can be time-consuming and emotionally draining. My opinion is that it is best to work through a studio or agent until you feel very confident of yourself and have made good contacts in the field.

The portfolio

A good portfolio is the key to getting the job you want, whether it is salaried or free lance. The portfolio will be judged first by your hand, which means your technique, the care and cleanness of your line and painting. Second in importance is your color sense. The designs in your portfolio should, of course, be as beautiful as possible and have a good overall look. The stylist will then feel that with direction, your designing will fit into the studio's line.

A complete portfolio should have twelve to fifteen good pieces. Each one should be important in terms of either a classic or current look. A variety of designs with different themes and layouts should be included to show your technical skills, layout ability, and color sense to insure that you will fit into many jobs.

PREPARATION OF THE PORTFOLIO

It is not necessary to have a fancy presentation for showing your portfolio. The designs should be presented in the same way they are shown in a studio. They should be squared off with a triangle and neatly cut. Then they should be matted on white mounting paper. Two sizes of mounts should be used: a large paper that fits medium to large-size designs and a half size for small designs. This procedure makes it easy for the interviewer to flip through the portfolio.

Do not paste the whole design on the mat. The proper way is to tip it onto the mount with rubber cement or double faced tape on the top. Center the design and put a small amount of cement or tape on the center and upper corners. and press down. This leaves the design loose on the bottom, which prevents creasing if the mounts are rolled up, and makes the designs easy to remove for remounting.

For taking your portfolio around, large manila envelopes with handles, and vinyl and plastic carrying cases are available and inexpensive.

Designs that are very large and do not fit on the mounting paper can simply be rolled and carried separately. If they are on rice paper and can tear easily, invisible tape should be put along all the edges on the back of the design.

It is a good idea to put your name and address on the back of your designs and/or mounts. You can purchase a rubber stamp for this purpose. Designs that have sets of color combinations to go with them should be mounted with the design on top and the colorings underneath. If the colorings are too large to fit on the mount with the design, they can be mounted separately. Summing up, the portfolio should be clean, neat, and arranged in order with the small mounts on top and the large ones underneath for easy handling by the interviewer.

If one or more of the designs in your portflio are in repeat, that is fine. However, it is possible most of them will not be in repeat (as discussed in Chapter 7). When asked about your repeat skills in an interview, be frank and say either you are confident or that you will need a little extra time and/or help on the first one or two repeats. Most people understand this, since it would be impossible to be an expert repeat artist on one's first job. After your first couple of repeats are successfully completed, you will feel like an old hand at it.

Looking for a job

Your portfolio is all set and you are ready to look for a job. Here are some sources:

1. Your local state employment office. In New York City, there is a special person in the professional division to place textile designers. It is a good idea to call for an appointment. After you are interviewed and your portfolio evaluated, you will be notified when an appropriate job becomes available.
2. The classifed advertisements in the major newspapers. Look under Textile Designer, Designer, and Artist.
3. Professional job agencies. There is a fee charged for these positions sometimes but it may be worth a try.
4. Converters and textile design studios in the yellow pages of the telephone directory. They are listed under those headings. Call and ask to speak to either the personnel department or the stylist in the studio.
5. Friends or contacts who work in the textile industry. You will find that most people are helpful. Many places that do not have job openings themselves, will recommend you elsewhere if they like your portfolio.

Do not be discouraged. In my experience, everyone with a good portfolio will eventually find a position. However, even with a good portfolio, some people get placed quickly and others, because of a slow season, bad timing, personality problems, and so on, can take a while to find a job. Keep trying.

Individual enterprises

There will be people using this book who want to develop their own craft or product and find ways to market it. If you have one-of-a-kind items, research the art galleries and craft shops in your area. There are many shows exhibiting textile arts: fabrics that are woven, painted, stenciled, and so on. You should contact boutiques and department stores. It is a good idea to call first and make an appointment with the buyer to insure that the person in authority will be there to look at your work.

If a one-of-a-kind item becomes successful, be prepared to take orders on it and duplicate it — perhaps with some differences to maintain your own interest and its individual look.

There are many local and regional arts and crafts fairs. Your work must be accepted by a panel of judges at some of them, and an entrance fee is required at most of them. Refer to the listing in the Bibliography under Craft Sources for further information.

Chapter two

Materials, supplies, and how to use them

Paints   TEMPERA AND GOUACHE

Tempera and gouache are the basic opaque paints used in textile designing. Each produces a flat, dull, opaque finish. Whereas gouache is made with a preparation of gum, and tempera is made with egg, both are water based and can be used interchangeably on a design. Their great advantage is that being opaque, they cover pencil lines, and one color can be applied over another without bleeding or changing.

Gouache and tempera are mixed thoroughly with water to thin them. They should be thinned just enough to achieve a creamy consistency: If too much water is used, the paint will be so thin the paper underneath will show through. If not enough water is used, the paint will tend to chip, especially if two or three coats are used. Also, it is hard to draw fine details with thick paint.

Light colors such as white and yellow tend to bleed

when they are put on top of a darker color. If this happens, simply apply another coat of paint. When opening a new tube of gouache or bottle of tempera, you may notice an oily film on top. Pour off this oil and thoroughly mix the remaining paint. Tempera and gouache can be used on all the papers recommended in this chapter.

Listed below are what I consider the minimum number of basic colors a designer needs. Many other colors can be purchased, but with either of the sets of colors listed below you can mix and match virtually any desired color. (See Chapter 6.)

Gouache
(Winsor and Newton Designers Gouache [in tubes] or any other reasonably similar brand)

1. Flame Red
2. Sky or Cerulean Blue
3. Lemon Yellow
4. Orange
5. Daffodil or Tiger Yellow
6. Permanent Green Middle
7. Bengel Rose (Grumbacher brand is the best)
8. Turquoise
9. Brown
10. Lamp Black (tempera may be substituted)
11. White (tempera may be substituted)

Tempera
(Rich Art Tempera [in jars] or any other reasonably similar brand)

1. Vermillion
2. Light Magenta
3. Spectrum Green
4. Spectrum Orange
5. Spectrum Yellow
6. Van Dyke Brown
7. Turquoise
8. Spectrum or Azure Blue
9. Prussian or Ultramarine Blue
10. Poster Black
11. Poster White

DYES: CONCENTRATED WATERCOLORS

Transparent dyes come in bottles labeled Brilliant Concentrated Watercolors or Radiant Concentrated Watercolors. These dyes are the opposite of opaque tempera and gouache paints because they are transparent; that is, one color applied on top of another will form a third color. Light shades are made by mixing the dyes with water, and all the colors can be mixed together to create other beautiful shades.

Dyes are concentrated and very brilliant, and for this reason caution must be used when mixing a color. The addition of a very small amount of one dye to another can quickly change the color.

Dyes can be used on all white or light-colored drawing papers. (Since dyes are transparent, they do not show up on dark grounds.) They are particularly brilliant when used on waxed rice paper, which is also transparent. A design with dyes on waxed rice paper and mounted on white paper appears very bright, airy, and luminous. Remember, a few drops of Non Crawl must be added to the dyes so they will adhere to the waxed rice paper.

Dozens of dye colors are available in bottles; however, the colors in this list will enable you to mix and match most of the shades you will need.

Concentrated Watercolors
(Luma or Dr. Martin's or any reasonably similar brand)

1. Tropic or Hot Pink
2. Cerulean Blue
3. Daffodil or Tiger Yellow
4. Lemon Yellow
5. Flame Red or Vermillion
6. Orange
7. Grass Green
8. Sepia
9. Turquoise
10. Navy Blue
11. Gray or Black

Here are some tips on applying dyes:

1. Don't be afraid of the dyes. They tend to be unpredictable but with practice you will be able to control them.
2. Concentrate on one area of the design and work rapidly, smoothing out the dyes as you paint so that overlapping of strokes is not apparent.
3. When it is necessary to stop painting to refill your brush, stop where the interruption will be least noticeable, such as a narrow space between motifs. This will allow you to pick up the color and continue painting with a miniumum of obvious overlap.
4. When you pick up an edge to continue painting, it helps to feather your brush, that is, to use the tip of your brush with a very light touch when you make the connection. You can also try to blot up the overlap of dye very lightly with a tissue or the tip of your finger.

5. If puddles of dye appear, use a dryer brush. Do not overload your brush with dye unless you are painting a large area.
6. When painting large areas use the full width of the brush by applying pressure on it. This will give you the maximum coverage with one stroke and minimize the overlaps.
7. Use the right size brush for the space you are painting. A No. 7 brush or its equivalent will help you work quickly on large areas.
8. Don't make picky little strokes. Try to cover areas, both large and small, with as few strokes as possible. Go back and smooth out the dye quickly while it is still wet.
9. Mix enough color to complete your design; you will not have to stop to remix and match the dye.

Paper

MASA WAXED RICE PAPER

Waxed rice paper is rice paper with a surface that has been treated with a smooth coat of wax, which makes the paper completely transparent. Pencil lines cannot be erased on waxed paper; therefore, your design should be worked out first on tracing paper. Tape the transparent waxed rice paper on top of the tracing, mix your colors, and you are ready to paint. If you want to redo a design, to improve it or change the colors, simply place waxed rice paper on top of the design and make your corrections as you paint.

Both dyes and opaque colors can be used on masa waxed rice paper. However, as I mentioned before, when a design is painted with transparent dyes on transparent waxed paper and put on a white mount, the colors appear exceptionally clear and luminous. Such designs have a much lighter quality than those painted in opaque gouache or tempera.

The choice of which paper and paint to use on a particular design is determined by the look you want to achieve. Always choose the most sensible and appropriate materials to get the desired effect. When you have had experience in using all the different materials, supplies, and techniques on many designs, such decisions will be easy to make.

TWEED WEAVE, GEORGIAN, AND BRISTOL DRAWING PAPERS

Tweed weave is a substitute for a paper called Georgian that was traditionally used for textile designing and is now more difficult to obtain. Tweed weave or Georgian is an off-white paper with a slightly textured surface that takes dye, tempera, and gouache very well. Bristol drawing paper is another good surface. These papers come in large sheets suitable for big designs.

BRISTOL DRAWING PAD

A drawing pad of white Bristol or similar paper with a slightly textured surface is inexpensive and can be used for small to medium designs in all paints. It is also smooth enough for pen and ink. A pad 14 by 17 inches is adequate. Papers with very slick surfaces should be avoided as they do not absorb paints well.

COLORED PAPERS

Many papers with slightly textured surfaces are available in colors that can be used as backgrounds for gouache or tempera designs. One such paper is Mi-Teintes. Dyes, of course, being transparent, cannot be used unless the paper is very light in color.

Brushes

HOW TO CHOOSE AND TEST A BRUSH

In textile design, the important features to look for in a brush are its resiliency and point. Before purchasing a brush, complete these two tests: Dip the brush in water and make sure the bristles shape into a good sharp point; test the spring in the brush by snapping the bristles back and forth with your finger. Any good art supply store will let you make these two tests. For purposes of comparison, ask to see a Winsor and Newton brush, Series 7. This is the best brush available for textile designing, but it is expensive, especially in large sizes. I usually suggest to students that when they are buying Winsor and Newton brushes, they buy sizes one to four in Series 7 and switch to Series 707 for larger sizes. Series 707 is cheaper and quite adequate.

Of course, there are other good brands of brushes, for example, Grumbacher, and the salesperson may suggest others. In choosing any brush, use the previous tests to guide you.

Remember that regardless of its size, a brush must come to a fine point for textile design. There are many designers who use a No. 7 brush to do very fine work. The difference in a small and large brush is the amount of paint that the brush holds. All good brushes, regardless of size, should make a point fine enough to draw small details. However, beginners often feel awkward using anything but a very small brush for tight work. If this is true of you, try a No. 2, or 3 brush. These small sizes are inexpensive, and you can buy several to see which size you can work with most comfortably. It is also convenient to have a selection of brushes. Working on a design, I often use five or six brushes, one for each color.

The hairs on a new brush may tend to separate, making it difficult to keep a pointed tip. The solution for this problem is to wet the brush and swish it around on a cake of soap. When a good lather is on the brush, form it into the best point you can get and let it stand upright overnight or for a day or two. This forces the brush into shape. When you are ready to use it, simply wash away the soap. Always work the brush into a pointed tip on a scrap paper before you paint with it. Eventually the brush will stop separating.

Always put away your brushes after cleaning them and rinsing them well in fresh water. Stand them upright on the handle in your brush jar. When you are carrying them around with you, make sure the tip is protected. Do not use a good brush to apply bleach, chemicals, or substances that are hard to remove. Save your old brushes or buy some really cheap ones for that purpose.

If a brush has a single hair at its tip that is annoying when you paint, do not try to cut it off because you will be sure to cut into the other bristles. The proper way to get rid of the hair is to burn it off with a match. Wet the tip slightly and shape it into a very sharp point. Hold the brush up to the light, keep the hair in sight, and pass the flame *very quickly* over it, so the flame just catches the tip. You can repeat the process, if necessary. If possible, watch some experienced person do it before you try.

HOW TO USE YOUR BRUSHES

When you start painting, have a piece of scrap paper at hand on which to test your colors and to work the brush into a point before painting. Rest your arm on the table and hold the brush firmly about one and one-half inches above the tip. The brush responds to the amount of pressure you put on it. You control the delicacy or thickness of a line by applying more or less pressure to the brush. With more pressure, the paint spreads and you cover a larger area. A fine line can be made with a light touch using just the tip of the brush. Do not try to paint a large area with a small brush.

The amount of paint on the brush is also important. Do not overload your brush for the area you are painting. If you are using dyes, the result of overloading will be puddles of color that have to be quickly picked up with a tissue or brush. If you use too much gouache on your brush, you will have great difficulty in pushing the paint around and maintaining a fine point. Too much gouache will also cause cracking or chipping, especially if a second coat is applied.

Pen and ink supplies

TECHNICAL DRAWING PEN

A technical drawing pen has a container which you fill with ink. The ink flows out evenly as you draw and produces a good fine line. Pen points start with No. 0000 (very, very fine). A variety of points can be used with one holder, but it is inconvenient to have to change points often. Since the points cost almost as much as the whole pen, most people work with a range of pens with various sizes of points to accommodate different designs. Use No. 0 or 00 for very fine lines and No. 1 for average lines. The biggest problem with technical drawing pens is that they clog up, so follow carefully the directions given for cleaning and caring for them. They come in many price ranges. I suggest buying pens that are inexpensive and not too complicated. The best pen in this category is the Koh-I-Noor Rapidograph. Permanent drawing pens such as Pilot ultra fine point (Sc-uf) can also be used.

CROW QUILL PEN POINT

I recommend learning to use the old-fashioned crow quill pen point in a holder. The crow quill gives great flexibility in fine-line designs. For instance, when changing ink colors you merely have to clean off the point and dip it into the new color. When the pen point clogs up, simply swish it in water and wipe it off carefully with a tissue. Another cleaning method is to scratch off the caked ink with a razor blade (a single-edged blade is safer.)

The price of the point is nominal, and the point will last a long time if you take care of it. One holder can be used for all points. I recommend a Joseph Gillot pen point No. 659. This point is very fine but hard enough so that when you draw a circle the nib does not separate.

As with a brush, the pressure put on the point determines the thickness of the line. Most fine-line textile designs require an even outline. The trick in acquiring a good, even pen technique is to rest your arm comfortably on the table, get a firm grip on the pen holder about one to two inches above the nib, and keep a steady pressure on the point as you move it smoothly on the surface of the paper. Do not dig into the paper. If you do, the point will tend to separate and spatter. It will also cause the line to have varying widths. Practice this pen technique, particularly for drawing flowers. A smooth paper is best for pen and ink work. However, papers like Tweed Weave and others that have a slight texture can be used. Waxed rice paper is a problem for many beginners because the pen tends to get caught on the paper. As you learn to work more smoothly with the pen, using a light touch on the surface of the paper, you will overcome this problem.

INK

Any good waterproof or permanent ink may be used for designing. Make sure the ink is waterproof; if it is not, dyes and colors will smear when it touches them.

Other supplies

PALETTES

Many kinds of vessels in which to mix paints are available. Small covered jars made of plastic or glass are useful. Other pallettes, made of plastic or porcelain, have six or eight recesses in which to mix colors. When using these you must cover the colors tightly with tape or plastic wrap when you stop painting. Put a couple of drops of water in gouache or tempera mixtures before covering them to compensate for any evaporation that may occur. There is nothing more annoying than starting to work and discovering that your paint has dried up. If this does happen, add a few drops of water, just enough to cover the paint, and cover the container tightly. In a short time, the paint will loosen up as you mix it. Be sure to sop up any excess water before mixing to avoid making the paint too thin.

Plastic egg crates and ice cube trays are also good cheap containers for mixing paint.

RULER

An 18-inch steel ruler is the best one to purchase. It will last forever and is long enough to measure large designs. Learn to measure accurately. I have noticed that many students think that one-half inch and one-quarter inch are the same thing. They are not, and one-quarter of an inch makes a big difference when you are laying out a set design or measuring a repeat.

TRIANGLE

A 12-inch plastic triangle can be used for both large and small designs. I usually start a design by squaring off my paper with a triangle. This serves two purposes: First, it gives the design an enclosure on the top and left side; it is usually not a good idea to work to the very edge of the paper because this leaves no space to extend the design if necessary. Second, the right angle forms a horizontal and vertical line from which a stripe or any set layout can be measured.

TRACING PENCIL

No. 3H or No. HB are good tracing pencils. Neat and clean tracings are of great importance. If the lead is too hard, the design will be difficult to see when the tracing is rubbed down. If the lead is too soft, the tracing and rubdown will become sloppy. Therefore, you should test several pencils and select the best lead for your hand, using No. 3H as a starting point. Keep your tracing pencil sharp to attain maximum clarity of detail. A sandpaper block or small pencil sharpener should always be near by when you work.

FELT-TIP MARKING PENS

Felt-tip marking pens are available in a great variety of colors and widths. Make sure you get a marker that is stamped either permanent or waterproof. If you do not use a waterproof marker to outline motifs that are colored with dyes, smearing will occur when the color is applied. To test the marker, simply draw a line on a piece of paper, wet your finger, and run it over the line; If it smears, do not buy it.

SOAP, KNEADED, AND PLASTIC ERASERS

Make sure the eraser is clean when you use it. Use a light touch when erasing pencil lines on gouache grounds so that you do not smear the colors. A plastic eraser works well on transfer-paper lines.

SPOON OR RUBBING BONE

You can purchase a rubbing bone with which to rub down tracings. However, an ordinary spoon will work very well. Put your thumb in the *bowl of the spoon and use the edge* of the spoon to rub down the tracing. You can also use a knife that is not too sharp-edged. (See Chapter 5.)

NON CRAWL OR WAX GRIP

Non Crawl is a liquid medium that is added to dye or paint to make it adhere to slick surfaces. Mix a few drops of Non Crawl in the color when you are painting on waxed rice paper, acetate, or any other surface that resists paint.

   Liquid soap may also be used as an adherent. A few drops of ordinary household soap in your dyes will serve the same purpose as Non Crawl. It is a good idea to try both Non Crawl and soap to decide which one works best on a particular design.

BLEACH

Bleach is used for creating special techniques when designing with dyes. It is also used to make corrections and touch-ups. (The use of bleach is explained in detail in Chapter 8.) Clorox is the strongest bleach.

ACETATE

A sheet of treated or plain acetate is invaluable for testing designs and colors before painting on your final paper. Treated acetate has a prepared surface that is nonresistant to paint. Plain acetate will require a few drops of Non Crawl in the paint or dye. Colors can be washed off the acetate, and the sheet can be used over again. Some studios find it convenient to use acetate for color combinations and other design work.

PRO-WHITE

Pro-white is an opaque white paint that covers a dye color without the latter bleeding through. It can be used to cover mistakes and make corrections or to put touches of white on designs painted in dyes. Pro-white is particularly effective in small areas; large areas covered with it can look messy. Pro-white can also be used in place of gouache or tempera white.

LIQUID MASK

A liquid masking medium can be purchased under a variety of names — among them Maskoid and Friskit. It is a thick, gray liquid that is applied on specific areas to mask them off from the rest of the design. This technique allows colors, such as grounds, to be painted on top of the areas that are masked off, and the area beneath the mask remains unaffected. The mask is then peeled off. There is a tendency for the edges of the motifs to appear blurry when the mask is peeled off. Therefore, the mask is best used on freely rendered designs rather than on tight ones.

Do not use good brushes when applying liquid mask. Wash the brush immediately after using. If necessary, clean it first with rubber cement thinner, then soap and water.

SARAL TRANSFER PAPER

Saral transfer paper is used to transfer a single motif or a whole design from tracing paper to drawing paper. The transfer paper is placed, *carbon side down*, on the drawing paper. The tracing paper, which has the motif or design on it, is laid on top. The motifs on the tracing paper are retraced in pencil and are transferred to the drawing paper underneath. Heavy pencil lines are hard to erase, so use a light touch when retracing. Use a plastic or kneaded eraser for transfer paper lines.

Transfer paper comes in different colors. White and yellow can be used on dark-colored grounds; graphite (gray) is good for light-colored grounds. However, do not use graphite or any other dark color when you are going to paint very pale colors on a light or white ground. In this case, work with a light-colored transfer paper so that the lines will be easier to erase after the colors have been applied. The use of Saral transfer paper is an alternative to the rubdown method described in Chapter 5.

RULING PEN

A mechanical pen used for ruling straight lines, a ruling pen has two sides that open and close by turning a small screw. Ink, paint, or dye is placed between the two sides with a brush or pen point and the screw is tightened to the width of the line desired. The ink flows out as the line is drawn against a firmly held ruler or triangle. Many people tape 2 or 3 coins on the back of the ruler to raise it above the surface of the paper, so that when the tip of the pen moves against the ruler, the fluid will not smear.

When a thick line is desired, it is best to draw two thin lines next to each other and fill in the space with a brush. Gouache and tempera should be watered to the consistency of India ink so that the paint will flow evenly out of the ruling pen. If the fluid dries in the pen and does not flow out, the pen must be dipped in water and thoroughly cleaned with a tissue. Fresh ink or paint is then placed in the pen. It is important to wipe off any drips on the sides of the ruling pen before you start drawing with it. Ruling pen lines are used for stripes, geometrics, and any other design that requires motifs with neat straight edges.

Chapter three

The importance of reference material

The importance to a designer of collecting and using good reference material cannot be overemphasized. A designer's career can easily span two or three decades, during which time thousands of designs may be worked on. Designs change constantly in style, theme, color, and technique; in order to keep up with these changes, you must always be alert for all kinds of reference material. This material can be gathered, for example, by clipping newspapers and magazines; collecting books, brochures, and swatches of fabric; and visiting museums, art shops, and galleries. Every artist's studio is filled with photographs, postcards, artifacts, and clippings of all kinds from all parts of the world. This material provides inspiration from art created by past and present cultures.

Originality is achieved when the artist either changes or combines things done in the past in accordance with his or her fresh point of view. For example, in designing a pattern with an old-fashioned Victorian bouquet tossed on top of a geometric Art Deco background, two pieces of reference material have been put together to create an original look.

The way designers use their reference material varies a great deal. Sometimes the reference sparks an idea in your head, and when the design is finished the connection between it and the reference is virtually unrecognizable. Other times, the connection is quite obvious.

It is not a good idea to copy a piece of reference material for a design without adding your own original touch. For one thing, many other designers may have acquired and used the same piece of reference. Occasionally, you are lucky enough to find a rare, original, or old piece of reference that you can be reasonably certain no one else has got hold of. In such a case, only minimal changes need be made in the original material for your design.

Uniqueness and originality

Students are always worried about being original. To allay these fears, I have made the following experiment many times in class: The students, perhaps thirty in all, are given specifications for a floral design, including the kind of flowers, the size of the flowers, the layout, and the color. To make it even more specific, I draw the design on the blackboard. Each student must then work out a design as outlined. You would expect to see thirty very similar designs. Instead, the results are invariably thirty different designs, no two of them identical. My conclusion: You do not have to worry about being unique and original. Each person has her or his own particular set of esthetic values that come into play when creating a design.

Developing your eye

The important thing for a textile designer, or any artist, is to keep developing a sense of design, layout, and color. To do this you must devote lots of time to looking at many different kinds of art, from current design magazines to antique Chinese porcelains. (See the following section, Where to Find Reference Material.)

When you look at a piece of art it can be appreciated on several levels. One is the emotional reaction you have to it. Another is the appreciation of the skill and meaning that the artist put into it. Then there is seeing it with a designer's eye, that is, extracting from the work of art the various elements that can be translated into design.

By consciously training yourself to see art in this way you are not only developing your eye but also storing up a great many visual ideas and concepts that can be called on when needed. You are training yourself to see spatial relationships (layout), color relationships (the way one color reacts when placed next to another), and ideas and concepts (creative imagination).

Where to find reference materials

BOOKS

In recent years, there has been a proliferation of art books of particular value to designers. A compilation of the best of these books is in the Bibliography.

MAGAZINES

There are many fashion and home furnishing magazines and they are good sources of reference for designers. They can be subscribed to or bought at newsstands, stationers, and book stores. Foreign magazines, such as those published in France and Italy, are expensive; therefore, I would thumb through them and purchase only an issue that contains a large amount of usable reference material. Magazines are especially good sources because they are current and have excellent color plates that can be clipped and filed for future reference. (See the Bibliography for magazine listings.)

NEWSPAPERS

The daily newspapers are another good source of current reference material. Many papers have special sections dealing with fashions, home furnishings, art, and design. There is coverage of the high-fashion showings in Paris, Rome, New York, and other fashion centers. These stories give clues to the latest styles, designs, and colors that will be copied and become popular.

There are also articles on the new trends in home decorating, such as sheets and pillowcases, wallpaper, furniture, and fabrics. News stories are printed about designers and current collections of fabrics, artists and crafts people, and where to find artworks that have been designed in all parts of the world.

Newspapers have reviews of books relating to the arts and design and listings of and features on all kinds of art and antiques in galleries, museums, and auction houses.

One newspaper subscribed to by all converters and design studios is *Women's Wear Daily*, which furnishes the fashion and fabric design world with the latest news. A weekly publication devoted to home furnishings, including textiles, is *HFD — Retailing Home Furnishings*. Both of these publications are available by subscription. However, I would not subscribe to them if I had contact with a studio or a converter where copies are available. (Addresses are in the Bibliography.)

MUSEUMS

Museums are a major source of inspiration and reference for artists and designers. There have been shows of Navaho rugs, Indonesian batiks, early American quilts, Chinese embroideries, African textiles, Japanese stencils, and Guatemalan weavings, to mention a few of particular interest to textile designers. Such shows are listed and often reviewed in newspapers and art magazines. Books and brochures with informative texts and reference material are usually available at the show. Always checks museum shops for catalogues, postcards, reproductions, and books; they provide new and excellent reference material for your collection.

There is often a direct link between a trend in design and an art show in a museum. An example of this is the Tutankhamen exhibition, on loan from the Cairo museum, which traveled throughout the United States in the late 1970s. As a result of the interest created by this show, the home-furnishing market, which includes towels, sheets, wallpaper, and drapery, was flooded with Egyptian designs.

Many museums throughout the world have special textile collections and they are invaluable sources of reference material. In most cases an appointment must be made to see the collection; when doing so, you should specify the kind of reference you want, in terms of type, period, and country of origin. Inquiries should be made about the museum's various facilities. For instance, museum collections may comprise fabric samples, a library of textile books, or a picture collection. They will usually have photocopy machines and allow you to make copies for your reference file. The major textile collections in museums in the United States are listed in the Bibliography.

FABRICS AND SWATCHES

Most department stores have fabric departments where apparel and home-furnishing fabric is sold by the yard. You can purchase one-quarter or one-half yard of a pattern. This is a good, inexpensive way to study designs with different techniques, colors, and layouts. A good exercise is to copy various elements of these fabrics to help you develop your hand. They can be used to inspire, and combined with your own ingenuity, to create new designs.

CARDS AND REPRODUCTIONS

Postcards, greeting cards, and art reproductions are inexpensive and convenient reference material in terms of size and handling. I recently saw a series of cards in beautiful colors depicting Japanese textiles. Look for florals, folk art, conversationals, and other decorative motifs when you visit card shops, book and department stores, and in particular, museum shops. The sales catalogues published by museums contain a good selection of cards and other reproductions that can be sent for by mail. (See the list of museums in the Bibliography.)

GALLERIES, AUCTION HOUSES, AND OTHER SOURCES

Designers often do not realize that a good way to build up an art background is to make use of the art galleries and auction houses in their vicinity. These places house a changing display of art and design from all over the world. The auctions are listed in the newspapers. The items for sale are put on display days before the auction. During this period it is possible to see and examine all these works of art.

Among the objects that can be seen in the art, antique, and craft galleries are contemporary and antique rugs, tapestries, quilts, embroideries, pottery, glass, porcelains, basketry, bead work, jewelry, furniture, paintings, and prints. Familiarizing yourself with this variety of visual treats will sharpen your design sense. If catalogues are not available, take notes and make sketches of items that suggest design motifs.

Flea markets are very popular all over the country, and interesting and affordable reference material can often be found there. At one such flea market, a student of mine recently purchased, for 14 dollars, a collection of large drapery swatches from the 1940s. Using them as a basis for design ideas, he created a successful series of wallpaper patterns.

Chapter four

Types
of
design

Each new season brings requests for different types of designs. The trends for the designs are developed from many sources. When the ecology movement gained prominence in the early 1970s, patterns called "landscapes," with sky, birds, water, trees, and so on, became popular. When a president went to China, "Oriental" designs were called for; when a Paris couturier had a gypsy theme for his new line, "peasant" designs were the vogue. The American bicentennial brought forth a wealth of "Americana." Whether the designer's inspiration is a museum exhibition or a social movement, the world of design is constantly changing.

Thus, a good designer must always be aware of the world and interested in culture and art, politics, and other current events. Of course, unless you are working as a free-lance artist, you are given the concept and very often the reference material by the stylist. The stylist is the person who styles the company's line for the season, and the one to whom the designer is responsible. The salespeople, along with the stylist, are in constant touch with the customers and the textile market. The designer's job is to translate the stylist's concept, with the help of reference materials, into a salable pattern that is esthetically pleasing.

A free-lance designer should give the collecting of reference materials top priority. It is always interesting to me to see how each designer will interpret the same reference in a different way, thus confirming my theory that we need not worry about being unique or different. We each have our own special way of seeing things, and textile designers, like all artists, must draw on past cultures to create a new look.

The list of designs in this chapter will familiarize you with a variety of classic and current patterns. The definitions are meant as a general guide to design types. Of course, they can be used in combination with new ideas, layouts, and colors to create a fresh look.

Floral

The floral pattern, in all its endless variations, is our most important basic design. Florals range from the smallest fine-line apparel designs to huge freely executed drapery patterns. Therefore, it is essential that every designer know how to draw flowers well, *and that includes the stems and leaves*. Most designers develop into good floral artists because they have had to trace and paint so many different flower motifs. From a good knowledge of flower drawing can flow a wealth of creative designs: abstract, stylized or realistic (as in Figure 4-1). Many techniques, such as shading, stipple, and dry

FIGURE 4-1:
A multifloral pattern with bright
colors on a dark background.
(*Brunschwig & Fils, Inc.*)

brush, may be used to achieve a realistic three-dimensional flower. (These techniques are described in Chapter 8.)

Florals are done in all layouts and all color schemes and can be combined with other motifs and nature subjects, as well as with many interesting backgrounds.

Folk

Folk designs (also known as *folkloric, peasant, ethnic,* and *provincial*) are inspired by the traditional popular motifs associated with specific areas or countries.

These motifs include all forms of plants, flowers, birds, animals, human figures, scenic subjects, and geometric patterns. The treatment of folk designs varies in each country — often highly stylized, sometimes quite realistic, surprisingly sophisticated, or delightfully naive.

Layouts can go wherever your imagination takes you and include all-overs (as in Figure 4-2), stripes, borders, and handkerchief squares.

There is a wealth of reference material available for this type of design since every country has its own folk tradition. Among the ethnic looks that have been used in the American textile market are Afghanistan, African, Chinese, Japanese,

FIGURE 4-2:   A decorative fabric adapted from Mexican motifs. (*F. Schumacher and Co.*)

American Indian, Russian, Egyptian, Indonesian, Mexican, Pennsylvania Dutch, Guatemalan, Peruvian, Persian, and Indian. See Color Plates 5 and 8, 12 and 13 for designs inspired by the art of some of these countries.

Colors can vary widely, from very bright and brilliant on dark or light grounds to earth tones and monotones.

Monotone

Monotones are designs using only one color with white, such as blue motifs on a white background (Figure 4-3a) or white motifs on a blue background (Figure 4-3b).

FIGURE 4-3a:
A navy-on-white monotone fabric.
(*Brunschwig & Fils, Inc.*)

FIGURE 4-3b:
The same design with the colors reversed to white-on-navy.
(*Brunschwig & Fils, Inc.*)

The absence of all but one color in a monotone design presents an interesting problem because there are no other colors to distract the eye. The background fabric forms a very noticeable pattern of its own. Therefore, the amount of design (known as *coverage*) becomes very important. It is a good idea to look at a monotone design from some distance to help see the color distribution.

Layouts can be as simple or complicated as you want and motifs or themes can be adapted from both modern and traditional sources.

A variation of a monotone occurs when the cloth is dyed a ground color first, say red, and another color, such as black, is used to print the motifs on top of it. The result is a two-color design, but the printing process is the same as for a monotone.

Patchwork

Patchwork designs are named for and derived from the early American quilts that were made by women in the eighteenth and nineteenth centuries. The usual patchwork quilt was made by cutting scraps and pieces of different printed fabrics and sewing them together to form beautiful geometric realistic or random designs. Another form of patchwork, called *appliqué*, is a technique of cutting the motifs out of fabric and stitching them onto a plain background to create a variety of complicated geometric and realistic designs.

Patchwork designs do not have to be made with traditional American motifs; they can easily be adapted from

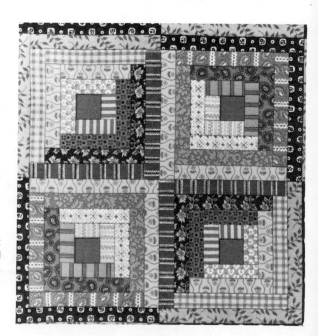

FIGURE 4-4:
A modern version of a traditional
patchwork design.
(*Brunschwig & Fils, Inc.*)

30

Oriental, African, or any other ethnic theme. Each area of a patchwork design should appear to be cut out of a larger piece of printed fabric. To achieve an appliqué look, the motifs should appear to be stitched onto the background. (See Chapter 5).

Although the colors in these designs are often bright, many subtle color combinations can be used. Why not a beautiful monotone patchwork? The size of these patterns can be from small blouse to large wallpaper and drapery, and layouts can range from very set (Figure 4-4) to free-flowing (See Figure 5-13 in Chapter 5).

Liberty

Liberty designs take their name from Liberty of London, an English textile company that used to specialize in blouse-size carefully drawn floral patterns. Today, however, Liberty produces many other designs as well. The classic Liberty floral design often has a fine-line outline.

The colors in these designs should be carefully thought out to add the most interest possible, and they can range from muted to bright according to current trends. Backgrounds can be any color, from white or beige to black. Layouts vary, with all-over packed (Figure 4-5) or spaced and stripes predominating. Liberties require a good tight hand and should be beautifully drawn. They should be small to medium in size, and as always, the florals can be combined with other motifs.

Liberties have become a classic in the American market.

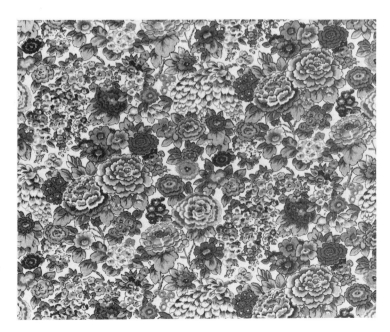

FIGURE 4-5:
A Liberty apparel design in a
packed floral layout.
(*Liberty of London, Inc.*)

Conversational

A conversational is a design with motifs that either tell a story or contain a message: In other words, it is a conversation piece.

This objective can be achieved by very realistic drawings (as shown in Figure 4-6) or by treating the subject matter so subtly that from a distance the pattern appears to be nothing more than a color effect.

Layouts can vary: all-overs, sets, stripes, borders, and so on.

Conversationals which are usually blouse size, can be campy and fun or sophisticated and high-style.

Care should be taken in the choice of motifs, color, and treatment to avoid mere cuteness. A good conversational can often be worn by both women and men and by all age groups. (See Figures 4-16 and 5-1a for other examples.)

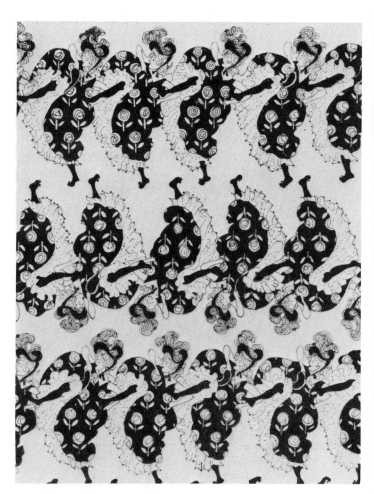

FIGURE 4-6:
A conversational apparel design in a two-way layout.
(©Carol Joyce)

Batik

Batik probably originated in China or India, although Indonesia, especially the island of Java, is most famous for it. Batik is a resist method of decorating fabric. Certain areas of the fabric are covered with liquid wax, and then the fabric is immersed in dye. The wax resists the dye in the areas that are covered. This procedure can be repeated many times to achieve the desired effect. In the dyeing process, a random crackle emerges where the dye penetrates the cracks in the wax. This gives batik its distinctive character (see Figure 4-7).

Javanese women make batiks either individually or collectively in small workshops. The traditional colors are browns and indigo blue, although today, all colors are used. Of course, we do our designs on paper and imitate the batik look (see Chapter 8), which is then simulated in roller or screen printing.

FIGURE 4-7:
A batik border design with a
Japanese fish motif.
(©Carol Joyce)

The layouts can be all-overs, stripes, and borders of all kinds. Motifs are usually traditional, such as Indonesian, Oriental, or African, and batik patterns can range in size from small blouse to large home furnishing. (See Figure 8-1 for another batik example.)

Chintz

Chintz is a glazed or polished cotton, usually used for upholstery and drapery fabric. The designs are florals with birds, figures, and so on. Chintz originated in the seventeenth century in India; therefore, the designs have a strong Eastern flavor. They are greatly favored by interior designers.

The layouts on chintz designs range from elaborate all-overs and stripes to very involved borders. Background colors can be white, off-white, black, or brights such as red, blue, and yellow. Any combination of rich or exotic colors looks well on chintz and is enhanced by the high glaze on the fabric. Beautiful drawing and painting are characteristic of chintz patterns (as in Figure 4-8). For another example of chintz design see Color Plate 7.

FIGURE 4-8:
A beautifully drawn chintz design with bright colors on a black background.
(*Boussac of France, Inc.*)

Geometric

A geometric design is made up of combinations of abstract shapes such as squares, triangles, and circles (see Figure 4-9). Geometric layouts run the gamut from large, spaced and free in feeling, to small, neat, mechanically set designs. Colorings in these designs range from monotone to bright and bold.

Geometrics are fine for anything from blouses to home furnishings. In recent years, the revival of Art Deco and the use of small neat patterns for home decorating have renewed the popularity of geometric designs.

FIGURE 4-9:   A geometric design in a one-way, tossed layout. (©Joan Nelsen, designer)

Foulard

A foulard (also known as madder, tie-silk, and cravat), a small neat design in a set layout, was typically used for necktie patterns. It is now used on apparel as well as home-furnishing fabrics. Foulards are carefully drawn geometric stylized floral, paisley, or Persian motifs.

These designs must be measured and laid out with precision, as in Figure 4-10. Ruling pen and compass should be used when needed.

The traditional colors include rich shades of red, blue, green, and gold, but all color combinations and backgrounds can be used. Foulards work well in all-over, stripe, and border layouts for both men's and women's wear.

FIGURE 4-10:
A typical foulard pattern.
(*Schwartz-Liebman Textiles*)

Art nouveau

Art Nouveau was an artistic movement that started at the end of the nineteenth century and ended about 1920. The movement was partly a reaction against industrialization and technologically reproduced objects. Art Nouveau design is characterized by sensuous, flowing, organic lines. Motifs are taken from nature and plant life. During the Art Nouveau period the famous Tiffany lamps and other beautifully designed home furnishings were produced. The Art Nouveau influence extended to textiles, architecture, wallpaper, furniture, ceramics, and many other areas, all highly appreciated today. Reference material for designers is plentiful. Beautiful muted tones combined with bright and dramatic dark colors can be used.

Layouts and sizes of patterns can vary according to the use of the design for either home furnishing, as in Figure 4-11, or apparel.

FIGURE 4-11:
A decorative fabric in Art Nouveau style.
(*Liberty of London, Inc.*)

36

Art deco

Art Deco is the art movement that came after Art Nouveau, lasting roughly from 1910 to the 1930s. A lot of its inspiration came from an acceptance of industrialization and the esthetics of machinery, stripping Art Nouveau of its ornament and flowing lines. Art Deco usually has geometric, angular, clean lines.

Dress fashions, accessories, architecture, textiles, painting, and ceramics were all part of the Art Deco movement. Motifs include flowers and other plant life (Figure 4-12), animals, human figures, and the geometric decorations of Egyptian art — all formalized, modern, and angular in execution.

Several shades of one color can be used, combined with creamy mauves, peach, grays, blues, and ecru (a yellowish beige) as well as brights on dark grounds. The size of these designs varies according to its use, either home furnishing or apparel. They tend to all-over set or spaced layouts. (See Color Plate 9.)

FIGURE 4-12: An Art Deco interpretation of a floral pattern. (*Clarence House Imports, Ltd.*)

Botanical

A botanical is a very realistic, well-drawn design using botanical motifs such as those found in illustrated books on plants, flowers, and herbs. The treatment is often detailed with fine-pen line and sometimes incorporates lettering to name the botanical species.

Color combinations range from pastel to bright. Botanicals range from small blouse size to large home furnishing (Figure 4-13).

Drawing technique is very important in this design.

FIGURE 4-13:   A botanical design on a dark background with bright florals. (*Boussac of France, Inc.*)

Toile (Toile de Jouy)

A toile design is composed of fine-line pictorial or scenic motifs. *Toile de Jouy* means "cloth from Jouy," and these designs originated in Jouy, a French town whose world-famous print works were founded in 1760. Stories, finely illustrated, of current events were depicted as well as romanticized landscapes and figures. Toile designs are traditionally used for classic home-furnishing patterns. Many museums and book collections have reference material on the old toiles, and many modern versions have appeared.

These designs are usually on neutral backgrounds with the motifs in dark fine-line drawing. Layouts are predominantly all-overs or stripes (see Figure 4-14).

FIGURE 4-14: "Steamboat Toile."
(*F. Schumacher and Co.*)

Stylized

A stylized design is one in which the motifs are abstracted or reduced to their basic shapes. Many florals and other nature subjects can be stylized to varying degrees and still remain recognizable, as shown in Figure 4-15. Art Deco is a good example of stylized design. All layouts and colors can be used for apparel and home-furnishing patterns.

FIGURE 4-15:
A design with a profusion of stylized
motifs.
(*The Cloth Company, Div. of Cranston
Print Works Co.*)

Americana

An Americana design is any design whose source is American history. The motifs can be symbolic (eagles, stars and stripes, etc.) or realistic (Pennsylvania Dutch and other folk art, including American Indian designs).

Colors can be bright and primary or monotone. They can be muted to effect an antique look or be traditional red, white, and blue. The layouts can vary as well as the size for either apparel or home-furnishing use. Figure 4-16 illustrates an apparel conversational design with Americana motifs.

FIGURE 4-16:
A two-way conversational design
for apparel with Americana motifs.
(©Carol Joyce)

Shirtings

Shirtings are designs with a neat tailored look, usually in a set or stripe layout, and traditionally used for men's shirts (see Figure 4-17).

Motifs can be combinations of paisley, floral, geometric, and foulard patterns. Colors can suit the current market, and size tends to be small. Tools such as ruling pen and compass are often required. Shirtings are a classic look used for women's wear as well as men's wear.

FIGURE 4-17:   A typical shirting stripe with floral and paisley motifs. (©Carol Joyce)

Landscape

Landscapes are designs in which the motifs are placed in a horizontal layout, and when combined with the subject matter, suggest a landscape.

Rural subjects such as clouds, birds, rainbows, animals, water, trees, and scenic motifs are used (see Figure 4-18). Colors range from pastel to bright. Landscape designs for apparel are done in blouse size, and larger for drapery, sheets, and pillowcases.

The drawing tends to be realistic, and a three-dimensional look can be created through the use of air brush, stipple, or other techniques. (For another landscape design see Figure 5-9.)

FIGURE 4-18: A landscape pattern with a nautical theme. (©Carol Joyce)

Country french

Country French designs originated in Provence, in the eighteenth century. They were printed from woodblocks by artisans. Gradually, motifs and influences from India and the Orient were adapted into the traditional Provence designs, although they retained a basic rustic look. Country French designs are often bright in color but other, more subtle, combinations can be used. They are often small and neat in layout, as in Figure 4-19, sometimes with beautiful borders, and are often designed to coordinate with each other for apparel or home-decorating purposes.

FIGURE 4-19: A collection of country French fabrics in bright colors on light and dark grounds.
(*Souleiado at Pierre Deux*)

Warp

A warp design is one that imitates the vertical yarns that are used on a woven fabric. (The horizontal yarns are called the weft). To imitate this warp look, you can draw vertical lines on and around the edges of the motifs with a pen line or fine brush. The result is a slightly blurred or stitched effect, as shown in Figure 4-20. (Also see Figures 8-13 and 8-14.)

Subject matter can range from geometrics to romantic-looking florals. Layouts and color combinations can vary widely, and warp designs are used for both apparel and home furnishing.

FIGURE 4-20: A bold warp stripe for the decorative market. (*Fabrics by Bloomcraft, Inc.*)

Paisley

Paisley is a design taken from the cashmere shawls of India that were woven in Paisley, Scotland. The paisley design is characterized by the palm or curved abstract figure, usually with elaborate symmetrical detail.

Paisley designs are sometimes very set in layout and conservative, but they can also be bold and dramatic in scale and design. Layouts are tossed, set, stripe, and border (see Figure 4-21).

Typical paisley colors are combinations of rich red, blue, green, and gold with brown and black. However, new and innovative color combinations can give a fresh look to the classic paisley design.

FIGURE 4-21: An elaborately detailed paisley design with a border. (©Carol Joyce)

Abstract

An abstract design (also known as contemporary or modern) is nonfigurative and usually has a modern crisp look. These designs can range in size from small apparel designs to large home-furnishing patterns. All color combinations and layouts can be used, although abstract designs often work well in spaced layouts. Figure 4-22 shows a drapery design painted with bold sweeps of a large brush forming a vaguely oriental stripe.

FIGURE 4-22: A large dramatic abstract drapery fabric.
(*Fabrics by Bloomcraft, Inc.*)

Coordinate patterns

A coordinate pattern (sometimes called a twin or companion print) is a design created with the same feeling as another pattern so that the two may be used together. Sometimes three or four coordinates are printed in a line of designs, making it possible to combine several for a coordinated look.

Coordinates can be made in many different layouts —stripes, borders, all-overs — and they also have coordinated colorways or color combinations. Often they are designed to contrast in layout and size, such as a small packed design with a spaced bold border design. A good coordinate print should not just be a duplicate portion of another pattern; it should hold up as a separate design on its own. (See Color Plates 9, 10, 12, and 13 for some good examples of coordinate patterns.)

Chapter five

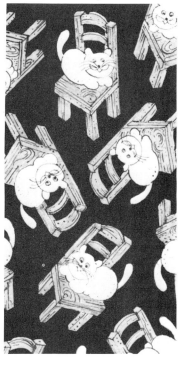

Designing
and
layout

Designing

Designing a textile requires a knowledge of layout, color, tracing, and painting techniques plus the proper use of materials, supplies, and references. There is no one way to start a design, but here is a general guide that will prove helpful.

The steps

1. Gather the reference material you plan to use for ideas and inspiration.
2. Make a small pencil sketch of the proposed design for an overall visual concept of it. Also write down color ideas.
3. Decide on the best paper, paints, and supplies to achieve the desired results in the easiest way.
4. Lay out the design on tracing paper. Double check the layout for balance.

5. Transfer the design from the tracing paper to the drawing paper (unless you are painting on waxed rice paper), using one of the methods described in this chapter. If the design requires a ground color, paint the ground on the drawing paper before transferring the design.

6. Mix the colors; put dabs of the colors next to each other on paper to see how they go together.

7. Paint a small square of the design in color to determine the best techniques to achieve the final look you have in mind. When this look is satisfactory, proceed with painting the design.

The importance of layout

There is probably no other art form that requires as thorough a knowledge of layout as does textile design. In textile patterns the design repeats itself on the fabric and must balance and flow smoothly in all directions. A poor layout will show up plainly on the printed goods, whereas an interesting layout can turn an ordinary idea into a good design.

Tips on laying out a design

1. There is no standard overall paper size required for a design. How large or how small you make your design depends entirely on the size of the motifs. For instance, a design consisting of very small flowers without any unusual color distribution, could require a painted area of only 3 by 4 inches. However, a design with a variety of large motifs in different colors might require 18 by 24 inches or more to be painted.

2. When you are starting to lay out a design, try to envision the overall layout so as to anticipate any problems that may lie ahead. Drawing a small sketch of the design first can be helpful.

3. Always think about the color distribution in your design. A plain black and white design might require an average-size layout, but the same design with an occasional red motif tossed in would require a layout large enough to accommodate the spacing of the red motif.

4. Look at your design from a distance to get a perspective on the layout. Hang it on a wall or look at it in a mirror — which reverses the design and gives you a different view of it.

5. Pay attention to small details when drawing or painting. For instance, the stems on flowers should be graceful and neither too long nor too heavy for the flower.

Tracing *The use of tracing paper*

1. To achieve a clean tracing line, always keep your pencil sharp. Draw single lines to outline the motifs. Do not use scratchy or double lines. The tracing should always be clean and clear.

2. When tracing, use a light touch. Do not dig the pencil into the tracing paper.

3. Always start a design with a piece of tracing paper larger than the size of the design you are doing. Do not start tracing on the edge of the paper. Leave a few inches all around to accommodate changes or additions and to avoid tears on the edges.

4. When creating a design, you can place motifs or groups of motifs in different positions on the tracing paper by using smaller pieces of tracing paper. First trace the desired motif on the smaller piece; then place it under the larger tracing layout, tossing or turning it in any position the design requires.

5. When the design is to be painted in dyes on waxed rice paper, always work out the completed design on tracing paper. When you are ready to paint, simply tape the waxed paper on top of the tracing paper and start painting. Pencil lines cannot be erased from waxed rice paper and will show through the transparent dyes.

6. When the design is to be painted in opaque colors (gouache or tempera), the way to transfer the design onto the drawing paper is to use the rubdown method described here or the transfer paper method described in Chapter 2.

How to rub down a tracing

A method that textile designers use to transfer single motifs or whole designs from tracing paper to drawing paper is called a rubdown. The motif or design is cleanly drawn on the tracing paper. *Top* is written on the front. The tracing paper is then turned over and "backed," which means retracing the motifs exactly on the reverse side. The tracing is then turned to the front and placed in the correct position to be rubbed down on the drawing paper.

The rubdown is done efficiently with the edge of a spoon

held in the thumb and forefinger. The thumb is placed in the *bowl* of the spoon, and the *edge* of the spoon is used to rub down the penciled motifs from the tracing to the drawing paper beneath. If the tracing appears too light on the drawing paper, you are not rubbing hard enough or you are not rubbing with the edge of the spoon. One tracing can be rubbed down over and over again until the motifs on the drawing paper are difficult to see. In this case you can retrace (or "back") the old tracing again or make a new one.

The tracing can be backed with white Conté crayon (keep the point sharp) when the rubdown is going on dark grounds. Other implements to use are a knife (not too sharp-edged) or a rubbing bone that can be purchased at an art store. See Saral transfer paper in Chapter 2 for an alternate tracing method.

Two-way layout

Apparel designs are usually done in what are known as two-way layouts (Figure 5-1a). In a two-way layout the design motifs go in all directions so that when the fabric is turned around or upside down, there is no discernable difference in the pattern. This type of layout minimizes waste of fabric when garments are cut. For instance, a dress manufacturer may buy thousands of yards of a two-way pattern, and after cutting a group of blouses, find some odd-shaped pieces of fabric left over; there will be no problem in matching motifs in the remaindered fabric to make, say, sleeves and collars. In a one-way layout (Figure 5-1b) the motifs in the fabric all go in

FIGURE 5-1a: A conversational design in a two-way tossed layout. (©Carol Joyce)

FIGURE 5-1b: The same design motif in a one-way set layout.

the same direction; therefore, leftover pieces of fabric are hard to match exactly, which can result in a lot of waste.

A two-way layout is usually less stiff that a one-way layout and, surprisingly, flows better. Most beginning designers are a bit thrown when called on to place a figure, house, tree, or animal upside down in a layout. However, after a short while it seems perfectly normal, as well as esthetically pleasing.

For home-furnishing designs, a one-way layout is usually suitable.

Types of layouts

The following are the most frequently used layouts in textile design.

ALL-OVER OR TOSSED

An all-over or tossed design is one in which the motifs are arranged in a variety of positions to achieve a tossed but balanced effect. The amount of space that the motifs cover on the background (known as *coverage*) can range from packed to spaced. A layout in which the motifs are placed very close together is called a *packed layout* (Figure 5-2a). A *spaced layout* shows a good deal of background (Figure 5-2b).

A good way to start a tossed all-over design is to lay out, or spot, on tracing paper the largest or most important motif or unit of design. Next, spot the second motif, and so on. The

FIGURE 5-2a: A floral design in a packed all-over tossed layout.

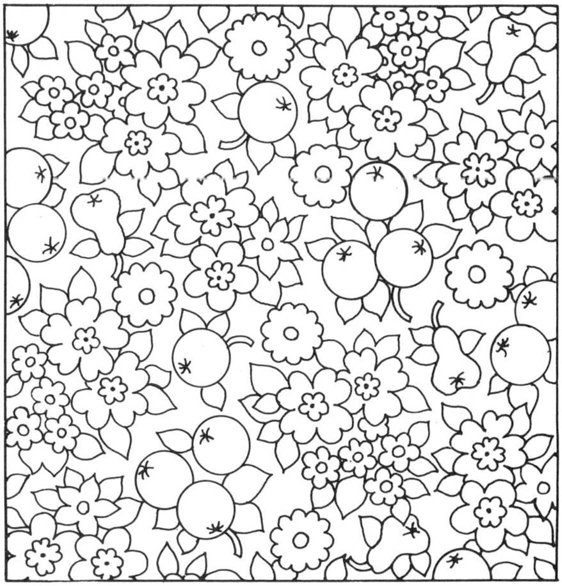

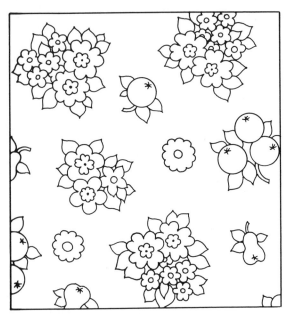

FIGURE 5-2b:
The same floral motifs in a spaced all-over tossed layout.

remaining background space can be filled in with the smallest motifs. To save time, circles can be substituted for the motifs (Figure 5-2c) and rearranged until you are satisfied with the overall layout. The circles can then be filled in with their corresponding motifs and the circles erased.

If there are spaces in the background that form paths running through the design without being interrupted by a motif, break up the path by rearranging the motifs. Motifs that form straight lines (known as *line-ups*) that look peculiar, or motifs that are so close together they cause a cluster in one area and holes in other areas, are all to be avoided. If these occur, redistribute the motifs until the overall layout appears balanced. Moving one motif may necessitate moving others until the design flows properly, so be aware of what is happening to the design as a whole.

When the design calls for a packed all-over layout, do not be afraid to have motifs such as leaves or flowers touch each other, appearing to wind under or over each other.

Your design should always give the illusion of a repeat, which is easily achieved by having all motifs, or as many as possible, appear more than once in the design. Do not forget the two-way look for apparel designs, unless a one-way look is specifically asked for. Either way, the more your finished design resembles a printed piece of fabric, the more confidence the customer or stylist will have in it.

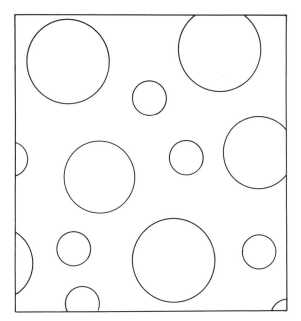

FIGURE 5-2c:
A tracing layout using circles to spot the motifs in Figure 5-2b. The motifs can be drawn in and the circles erased when the layout is perfected.

When you are satisfied with the layout on tracing paper, you are ready to decide the best way to execute your design, that is, which materials, paper, paint, and so on to use for the look you want. (Chapter 2 contains a complete discussion of materials.)

Your next step is to decide on the colors to be used and to test them on a small croquis (a corner of a design). Coloring is explained in detail in Chapter 6.

FREE-FLOWING

All designs must have a sense of balance; some of them are evenly spaced but others have a lot of flow and movement. Free-flowing designs must be laid out on a large piece of tracing paper and you must learn to use your eye to space (or spot) the elements of the design. Don't be afraid to place motifs on top of or underneath each other or wherever necessary to create the flow and movement desired. Start by sketching in the first motif, as in Figure 5-3a. Then sketch in the second motif, as in Figure 5-3b, and lastly, toss the other motifs, as in Figure 5-3c. Once you have finished spotting the overall layout, you can go back, take a fresh look at it, and make any changes necessary to improve it. Then you can perfect the drawing and add details.

FIGURE 5-3a: The first motif sketched in a free-flowing design.

FIGURE 5-3b: The second motif added to the layout.

FIGURE 5-3c: The third motif tossed on top to complete the design.

STRIPE

A design in a stripe layout must be carefully planned, measured, and laid out. Always use a triangle to square off a design (the triangle gives you an exact right angle from which to measure the widths of the stripes with your ruler). Whether the design uses a tight ruling pen stripe (Figure 5-4) or a free flowing one (Figure 5-5), measure the stripes precisely or the design will be crooked. Any combination or variety of widths can be used in a stripe design. For details on stripe repeats, see Chapter 7.

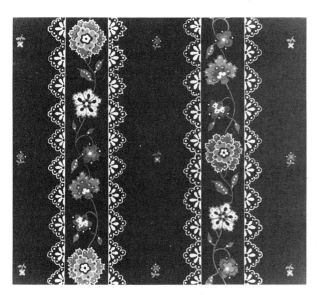

FIGURE 5-4:
A set stripe designed with the motifs confined within the ruling pen outlines. A lace effect is used on the edges of the stripe. (©Carol Joyce)

FIGURE 5-5:
Another stripe, but one that is interpreted in a looser and more free-flowing layout.

BORDER

Borders are some of the most versatile layouts. A border design can range in scale from a small blouse pattern to a huge sheet or drapery design. The border can be placed on one or both ends of a design. The remainder of the printed fabric above the border is called the *field*.

The border can be heavy and very important, with the field much lighter in feeling. Figure 5-6 shows a pattern with a wide, uneven elaborate floral border that covers a good portion of the width of the fabric, completely dominating the field. The reverse can be equally interesting: In Figure 5-7, a very elaborate field is accompanied by a narrow, rigidly confined border. For details on border repeats see Chapter 7.

The motifs in a set border or field must be carefully planned and meausured with a triangle and ruler. A more freely drawn border is also started by making a right angle with a triangle on the bottom of the tracing paper. This will give

FIGURE 5-6:
A border design wtih a wide, irregular floral border flowing into a field of small, scattered flowers. (*Schwartz-Liebman Textiles*)

FIGURE 5-7:
A border design with an elaborate, wide field that dominates a set, regular border. (*Clarence House Imports, Ltd.*)

you guidelines from which to measure the motifs, as you must make sure the elements are not crooked. Draw the right angle a few inches above the bottom of the paper so that the motifs will not be cut off at the bottom and there is room for a hem.

The border can also be placed on both ends of the fabric, either the same border or two different ones, as in Color Plate 11. Borders are often used in designs for sheets, pillowcases, and comforters (see Color Plate 6). Chapter 7 shows how to design a border in repeat.

SET

A set layout is one in which the motifs are repeated in exact measured spaces. (Figure 4-10 and Figure 5-1b are good examples.)

There are two ways to work out a set layout. One is to complete the design on tracing paper and then transfer it to the drawing paper. The second method is to work out the design directly on the drawing paper.

To work out a set layout using the first method, place a piece of graph paper of the correct measurement under your tracing paper and use it to calculate the spaces between the motifs in the design. Another way is to measure your own grid, or graph, on tracing paper to the exact size your design requires. This is done with a triangle and ruler, of course.

To save time and assure uniformity in drawing the motifs, only one or two neat renderings of the motif need be drawn on a smaller separate piece of tracing paper that has register marks on it. This can be aligned underneath the tracing paper grid, as shown in Figure 5-8, and moved about and traced as many times as necessary to complete the layout. Use a sharp pencil and do a neat tracing. If precision is required in rendering the motifs, use a ruling pen (see Chapter 2). Precise circles require an ink compass, which can be used with ink, paint, or dye. When the layout is complete, use either the rubdown method or transfer paper to transfer it to the drawing paper.

For the second method, a grid is drawn directly on the drawing paper, or a simplified version of a grid consisting of register marks is drawn lightly on the paper. It is a good idea to use register marks on paper that is not easily erased, such as painted opaque grounds. Again, only one or two neat renderings of the motif need be drawn on tracing paper that has register marks on it. The motifs on the tracing paper can be aligned with the drawing paper grid, moved about, and rubbed down as many times as needed. On dark painted

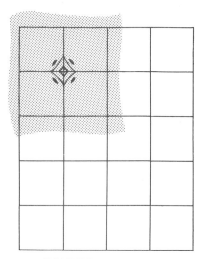

FIGURE 5-8:
A motif drawn on tracing paper (dotted area) and aligned on drawing paper grid in position to either trace or rub down.

grounds, go over the register marks with white paint or white Conté drawing pencil so they can be seen through the tracing paper. Set designs can be easily laid out in repeat.

LANDSCAPE

A landscape design is worked on a horizontal layout, as in Figure 5-9. These designs simulate a scenic landscape of various outdoor themes. They contain motifs such as sky, water, ships, trees, houses, flowers, and animals.

When you do a landscape design for apparel the size is from small to medium. For home furnishings the scale is usually large.

First, rough in the horizontal lines in the spacing required. Next, lay out the largest or most important motif or group of motifs well balanced on the paper. Balance in the second most important motifs and so on. Turn some of the motifs around if a two-way look is necessary. Try to envision the overall look, not just the individual motifs, as you lay out the design.

Don't forget: To help with your layout, you can simply draw in circles where the motifs belong and then trace the motifs in when you are ready.

FIGURE 5-9:
A design in a two-way landscape layout inspired by a Japanese wood-block print.
(©Carol Joyce)

HANDKERCHIEF SQUARE

A design with a handkerchief square layout looks like a number of bandanas or handkerchiefs, each with its own border, attached in a continuous pattern. The layout can be on a diamond, as in Figure 5-10, or a square, as in Figure 5-11.

Do the layout as you would any set pattern, using a triangle and ruler.

FIGURE 5-10: A handkerchief-square design worked in a diamond layout, inspired by traditional Asian motifs.
(©Carol Joyce)

FIGURE 5-11:
A handkerchief-square design
in the country French look.
(*Souleiado at Pierre Deux*)

PATCHWORK

When you are doing a design with a traditional or set patchwork layout, as in Figure 5-12, follow the rules for set layouts by making a graph of the required spacing for your design.

When you are creating a patchwork design with a swingy or tossed layout, as in Figure 5-13, the outlines of the large shapes should be laid out first on tracing paper. In both cases, the small patchwork motifs can be created and laid out on separate pieces of tracing paper. These tracings can then be placed in position under the grid on the large tracing and the patchwork designs filled in.

To achieve an authentic patchwork look, each patchwork section in the design must appear to be cut out of a larger piece of printed fabric. Therefore, the motifs must be traced and painted right up to the exact edges of each patch (Figure 5-13).

If an appliqué look is desired, you can simulate stitching around the edges and on top of the motifs to make them appear as if they are cut out of a piece of cloth and then sewn onto the background. (Figure 8-16 shows a design with this look.)

FIGURE 5-12:
A patchwork design inspired
by American quilt motifs.
(Waverly Fabrics, Division of
F. Schumacher and Co.)

FIGURE 5-13:
A modern patchwork design in a tossed
flowing layout. The flower and butterfly
motifs in white stand out against the heart-
shaped patchwork areas.
(©Carol Joyce)

Chapter six

Working with color

The importance of color

The way a design is colored is very important. A mediocre design can be made into a good one with beautiful color, and an excellent design can be spoiled with the wrong colors. Many converters hire artists, called colorists, who do nothing but color patterns.

Every pattern is printed in several different *color combinations*, also called *colorways* and *colorings*. These three terms are interchangeable, but for convenience in this book, I will use colorways, which is the term used in the home-furnishing market. The number of colorways printed of each design varies from three to many, depending on the stylist's decision. Sometimes, especially if a design is successful, it is recolored for a new season or for putting additional combinations in the line.

A colorway is a small squared-off portion of a design, large enough to contain all the colors in the design. The same squared-off section is used for each different colorway. They usually are painted on the same paper as that used for the original design. Some studios prefer you to place acetate on top of the design and paint the colorways right on the acetate. However, be aware that the colors tend to look different on acetate than they do on paper.

Waxed rice paper, because it is transparent, can be placed directly on top of the design when you are doing colorways. When painting on opaque papers, you have to make and rub down a tracing of the colorway (see Chapter 5) or use transfer paper (see Chapter 2).

When you are mixing colors for colorways, it is a good idea to paint small dabs of each color on a test paper to see how they work together. This is the time to make changes in the colors (e.g., darken or lighten them) before using them in the final colorway.

A roller or screen is made for each color in a design. Apparel designs usually use up to five or six colors. Home-furnishing patterns may use many more. When you are working out colorways on a pattern, the stylist will usually give you references, such as color tabs or a swatch of material to match. (See color matching in this chapter.) At other times, you will be given just the key, or main, color in each new combination. And sometimes you will be responsible for selecting all the colors, after being told the general color look desired in a particular pattern, for instance, two primary colorways and one neutral.

In all these cases, whether you are given complete or partial directions, begin by studying the color relationships in the original design you are working from. These color relationships will furnish the clues to the new combinations.

I have devised a chart to assist you in working out colorways. Please study the floral design and chart in the color section (Plate 2). The chart shows a set of three colorways worked out for the design. The use of the chart to work out your colorways (explained in the instructions that follow) will help you to analyze the color relationships in your designs and to make decisions about new combinations.

Color Chart   *How to work out the color chart*

1. Draw a chart as shown in Color Plate 2. In column 1, list all the colors in your design in the order of their importance. Try to list the colors that relate to each other (such as orange and yellow) directly under each other. This will be an instant reminder to keep this same

relationship when using substitute colors in the new combinations.

2. Head columns 2, 3, and so on, with the key color for each of the new combinations. Referring to the original design and using column 1 as a guide, work out in column 2 the first new colorway. Then work out the second colorway in column 3 and so on.

3. Because you have used a color in one colorway does not mean you cannot use it, or a different shade of it, in another colorway. However, be careful that the duplication of colors does not result in two colorways in the same set that are too similar in feeling.

4. A screen or roller is made for each color in the design. Therefore, make sure that if, for instance, you substitute blue in the new colorway for orange in the original, the blue *always* replaces the orange.

5. If you use different tones of one color, for example, a light blue and a dark blue, each tone counts as a separate color (except where a color goes from dark to light, in the technique known as shading).

6. The outline color on a design counts as a color. The outline color does not always have to be black; you can use brown, navy, gray, sepia, and so on.

7. If you feel your colorway has become either too bright or too muted, try combining two or three bright colors with two or three neutral colors to balance the colorway.

8. Experiment with unconventional ideas: Leaves do not always have to be green; they can be gold, rust, beige, blue, or any color that enhances the design. Also keep in mind that there are many shades of green, and using either bright primary green or a muted olive green for a leaf color can make a difference.

9. The colors you list in the color chart are only a guide. Sometimes, after mixing a desired color, you will find it doesn't work on the colorway. Then simply refer back to the chart and rethink that color. Sometimes when one color is changed, other colors have to be adjusted.

10. Sometimes, all the colorways in a set are done in the same values and intensity as the colors in the original design. At other times, one or two colorways in a set are weighted to the original colors, and one or two different looks are included.

Color matching and mixing

Mixing and matching colors in opaque gouache and trans-parent dyes is one of the most important skills required to produce good color combinations. You will be called on to match colors from color tabs or chips, from swatches of fabric and other painted designs, and from assorted scraps and clippings of all kinds. Many of the graphic arts have developed rules for the use of primary and secondary colors. However, these rules do not always work when applied to textile designing.

Each design has its own color problem. The amount of coverage of each color, the amount of background color, the layout and spacing of the motifs, and many other subtleties all make a difference in how the colors in each design relate to each other. Sometimes, to create a new look you want to combine colors that would not ordinarily go together. Each design should be approached on an individual basis, empha-sizing what I describe as the overall color feeling. If the distribution of the colors in your design looks unbalanced, a separate tracing overlay can be made for each color. Simply use circles on each overlay to indicate that particular color. Study the overlays and respot the colors that are too crowded together or too sparsely represented. (See Color Plate 4, a, b, c, and d for examples.)

TIPS ON MIXING AND MATCHING
COLORS WITH GOUACHE AND DYE PAINTS

The best way to learn how to mix color is to experiment with coloring your own designs. As a start, here are some basic rules for mixing color.

1. Use a vessel large enough to hold the total amount of paint you will require to finish your work, plus a small amount for possible touch-ups.
2. When mixing a shade of dye, imagine a scale of one to ten, ten being the strongest color, straight from the bottle (see Color Plate 3). As a general rule, if the strength of the tone you are matching is five or below on the scale, start mixing with water and then add the dye. If you start with the dye, which is extremely concentrated, you will have to add water endlessly to arrive at the desired lightened color. This is not only frustrating but also

wasteful, as you will probably end up with much more color than you need.

If the tone you are mixing is above five on the scale, start mixing with the dye and then add water until you get the desired shade.

3. When mixing dyes, start with the bottle of color that is closest to the color you are trying to get; then add the other colors needed to arrive at the exact shade. Use water to lighten, if necessary. Remember that concentrated dye colors are very powerful. When even a drop of a new dye is added to a color, the shade will change rapidly. For example, if you want to tone down hot pink, just a touch of yellow will do it: Too much yellow will make the pink too orangey. It is best to be careful and add too little rather than too much. You can always add more if needed.

4. When matching a color with opaque gouache or tempera, use white to lighten the color. Mix the paint with just enough water to obtain a creamy, smooth consistency that covers flat and opaque when applied to the paper.

5. Matching a color is a trial-and-error process. Here is a method to test a color for a match: After mixing the color, put a dab of it on the edge of a scrap of the same kind of paper that the colorway is on. Let the color dry thoroughly (because wet color is very different from dry color), and then place the color chip directly on top of the color you are matching. This will give you an instant comparison. You will immediately see whether the color you are mixing is too light or too dark and so on.

If a change has to be made, add the colors necessary to correct the shade. Make another test dab, let it dry, and repeat the comparison process. You may have to do this many times before you are satisfied that you have matched the color.

6. Many stylists are very picky about matching colors; others are more casual. It is best to be picky yourself and develop high standards.

How to make colored grounds

Many colored papers are available to use as backgrounds for designs. However, there is no substitute for knowing how to make your own colored grounds. For one thing, many times a specific background color has to be matched and used for a design or a colorway, and no such colored paper is available.

It is necessary for you to be able to produce any ground color of any size yourself, when working at home or in a studio.

Tips for making grounds

1. The vessel you use should be large enough to hold enough paint for two grounds. This will give you a backup ground in case of mistakes. Save any leftover paint for touch-ups.

2. Try to find a 3 or 4 inch inexpensive natural bristle ground brush at an art supply store. If this is not possible, pick out a good natural bristle brush of this size at a hardware store. A 1 or 2 inch brush is good for small grounds.

3. Other tools can be used to paint grounds, among them a small roller and flat foam rubber brushes of various sizes. These can be purchased inexpensively at a hardware store and are worth a try, although I like a brush the best.

4. Do not paint to the edges of the ground paper unless it is taped or tacked down. Leave about 2 inches of un-painted edge on all sides of the paper or it will curl up, making it difficult to handle. Lay scrap papers under the ground paper to avoid mess, and have a large water container at hand. You are now ready to apply the ground.

HOW TO APPLY THE GROUND COLOR WITH OPAQUE PAINTS

One method is to dip the slightly moist brush into the paint mixture and apply the paint with even strokes across the paper and then up and down. Moisten the brush as needed. An alternative method is to first put a very thin coat of water on the paper. The water will help the paint to spread over the ground paper. The trick is to brush quickly and evenly until the ground looks smooth. Work from top to bottom and then from side to side or vice versa.

During the process, more paint or water can be added as needed and brushed smoothly into the ground paper. At the end you can feather the brush strokes, which means to smooth out the ground lightly with the tip of the brush. Put this ground aside to dry and start the second one. If a ground does not dry smoothly, do not waste time doing a design on it; use the second ground or make a new one. Not enough paint has been applied if light streaks are showing through the ground color. Too much paint has been applied if the ground appears thick and grainy.

HOW TO APPLY
THE GROUND COLOR WITH DYES

The same general rules apply when using dyes as when using opaque paints. However, transparent dyes get deeper in tone as each additional coat is brushed on. Therefore, test a small area first, brushing back and forth. If the test ground dries too dark, add water to the mixture and test again. When the test area dries to the desired shade, the dye is ready to use.

When painting the ground, do not let the dye dry; work fast, brushing back and forth with even strokes, vertically and horizontally.

How to paint a blotch

A blotch is a term used to describe a background color that is painted around the motifs in a design. A blotch is applied in the background after the motifs have been completed. Blotching can be done in both gouache and dye colors. However, it is easier to paint around the motifs with flat opaque paints than with dyes; therefore, I often paint the motifs in dyes and then use gouache for the blotch background. Dyes may show overlaps and create an uneven background, particularly when you blotch a large area. Small areas generally do not present problems. However, at times it is necessary to blotch large areas with dyes, so it is a good idea to practice this technique. (See Chapter 2 for tips on applying dyes.)

If a dye blotch is unsatisfactory, match the color (or mix an entirely new one) with gouache or tempera and simply apply a coat on top of the dye. A tight blotch is painted right up to the edges of the motifs, as in Figure 6-1. A blotch painted loosely around the motifs, as in Figure 6-2, creates a more casual effect by leaving white randomly around the motifs.

Blotching is a good alternative to painting the design on colored ground. The advantage of the blotch method is that you can draw fine outlines and paint colored motifs in dye or gouache on white paper before adding the background. The blotch technique can also be used to enhance a design by creating white motifs in the background spaces. Before applying the blotch, consider the possibility of leaving white areas unblotched for motifs, such as groups of small flowers and vines. This is done by sketching and tracing the new motifs in the background in a balanced fashion and then

Plate 1 (previous page)
In this design the dark green ground was painted first in dye. Next, the black outlines were drawn in water-proof ink. Bleach was then applied to all the motifs to make them white. Finally, red, blue, and yellow dyes were used on the motifs. Some white motifs were highlighted with yellow and others left all white.

See Chapter 8 for Bleach Techniques.

© Carol Joyce

A

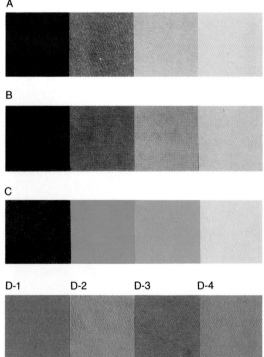

B

C

RED	BLUE	BROWN	PURPLE
ORANGE	AQUA	RUST	FUSCIA
GOLD	MAUVE	BEIGE	PEACH
LIGHT GREEN	OCHRE	LIGHT TEAL BLUE	LIGHT OLIVE GREE
DARK GREEN	BROWN	DARK TEAL BLUE	DARK OLIVE GREE

Plate 2 (above)
The chart shows a set of three colorways worked out for the floral design above. The colors in the design are listed in Column 1. The corresponding new combinations are listed in Columns 2, 3 and 4.

Refer to Chapter 6 for instructions on How to Work Out a Color Chart.

© Frank Delfino, Designer

D-1   D-2   D-3   D-4

E

Plate 3 (left)
A chart of dyes (concentrated water colors). A, B and C show different shades from undiluted dye to a tint as more water is added. D-1 is grass green, D-2 is orange, D-3 is grass green mixed with a small amount of orange, D-4 is orange mixed with a small amount of grass green. E shows various shades of purp and blue made by mixing hot pink and turquoise. The shades are lightened with water.

(a) Primary

(b) Neutral

(c) Bright Pastel

(d) Monochromatic

Plate 4 a-d

A group of colorways showing a design done in four different color treatments.

Frank Delfino, Designer

te 5 (left)

pparel design inspired by
ainian folk art. The motifs in
ary colors are effectively set off
he black background.

rol Joyce

te 6

eet, pillowcase, and comforter
a wide dramatic border and a
of small tossed flowers and
es.

antry, a Martex pattern by Lynn Johnson

te 7 (bottom)

aditional glazed chintz home
ishing fabric on a jade ground.
motifs are very well drawn and
anced by shading and stipple
k.

talia, Brunschwig & Fils, Inc.

Plate 8 (left)
A beautifully detailed fabric
adapted from traditional Persian motifs.

Hassan, Brunschwig & Fils, Inc.

Plate 9 (above)
A design showing Art Deco influence
in a spaced all-over layout for apparel wear.

The Cloth Company, Div. of Cranston Print Works Co.

Plate 10 (right)
The coordinate pattern has the same motifs,
smaller in size, in a packed all-over layout.

The Cloth Company, Div. of Cranston Print Works Co.

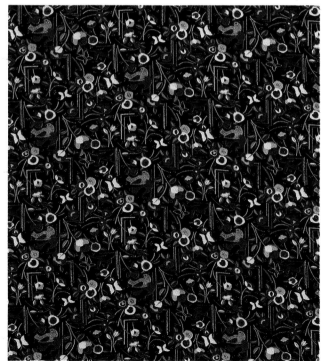

Plate 11 (bottom left)
This apparel fabric is designed utilizing the full width
of the cloth. A different border on each selvage
creates an unusually dramatic look.

The Cloth Company, Div. of Cranston Print Works Co.

Plate 12 (top right)
A bold home furnishing fabric inspired by traditional
Afghanistan motifs.

Pomegranate, Jack Lenor Larsen, Inc.

Plate 13 (bottom right)
The coordinate stripe pattern is done in the same bold
technique.

Bukhara, Jack Lenor Larsen, Inc.

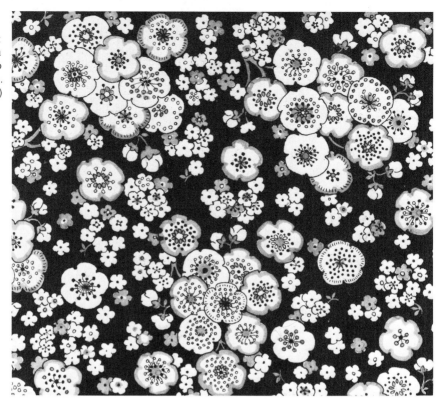

FIGURE 6-1:
A floral design with a
tight blotch painted to
the edges of the flowers.
(©Carol Joyce)

FIGURE 6-2:
A floral design showing
blotch painted loosely
around the motifs
creating a random effect.
(Fabrics by Bloomcraft,
Inc.)

proceeding to blotch around them. Touches of color can then be added to these motifs or they can be left all white.

How to paint a ground on the back of a design

On waxed rice paper, which is transparent, a ground can actually be painted on the back of the paper after the design has been completed. To do this, turn the design over, face down, and paint the ground on the back. Both dye and gouache can be used. The wax forms a protective coat so the colors on the front will not bleed. Keep the color of the ground light so any change in the colors on the front is minimal. Test the ground color on a scrap of paper first to see how it looks when viewed from the front.

If you do have to use a dark ground on the back, use the blotch method so that the colored and white areas on the front will not be affected. If a ground is painted in dye on the back of a design on waxed rice paper and white motifs or areas are required on the front, they can be created by using bleach (see bleach techniques in Chapter 8).

Chapter seven

How to put a design in repeat

What is a repeat? Understanding a repeat and its relationship to the printing process will prepare you for the step-by-step guide for working out a repeat that follows later in this chapter.

The unique characteristic of textile design is that unlike other commercial art forms, the design must be prepared to be printed over and over again in a continuous flow, without any apparent interruption in the pattern. The rendering of this artwork in a predetermined measurement is called a repeat.

Every design must be put into repeat before it can be printed. This means that the motifs in the design must be organized in a balanced layout that fits into an exact measurement so that repetition of the design will not overlap in the printing process. When it is finished, the repeat is sent to the textile printing plant where a separate screen or roller is prepared for each color, and the design is then printed on the fabric. When a repeat is done properly, a beautiful smooth-flowing pattern appears on the fabric with no discernible trace of a repeat line.

The two main printing methods are copper roller printing and screen printing. In all methods, the preparation of the repeat is the same. (See Chapter 9 for details of the printing process.)

Since every design must be put into repeat eventually, why not simply put every design in repeat to start with? The main reason is that it is faster and easier to concentrate on creating a beautiful design when unencumbered by the technical demands of the repeat. Moreover, the stylist often makes changes on the original design, and these changes have to be incorporated into the repeat. When you are free-lance designing, you obviously cannot know the exact repeat size that the purchaser requires. You may spend a great deal of time creating the original design in repeat, only to find that a different size is required or that some motifs or colors have to be changed.

Therefore, a design is usually created in a layout that gives the illusion of a repeat. When successful, this results in a design with a repetition of motifs in a balanced layout that are not actually measured out in repeat, but appear to be. It is only after all the decisions have been made about how the design is to be printed that the actual repeat is worked out. Sometimes a slightly new version of the design must be created in order to incorporate all the desired changes in the repeat. However, the changes usually do not appreciably alter the original design, so do not be upset at making them. The design is still basically yours, and occasionally the changes may improve it. Sometimes the repeat on a pattern is done by its designer, and at other times by a repeat artist.

All this does not mean that you never design in repeat. There are times when designing directly in repeat is required or makes sense. One of these times is when you are working in a salaried job and all the pertinent repeat information is supplied to you by the stylist. For example, the stylist might approve a sketch for a design that is laid out in a pre-determined repeat size; then your job would be simply to continue it and paint it to completion. It also makes sense to design in repeat when you are creating a pattern in a set layout such as a stripe, border, or other design that must be laid out in exact measurement anyway.

It may surprise you to learn that every design, even one that looks odd or very complicated, can be put into repeat with the proper manipulation of the motifs. Always remember to keep as much of the original design as possible in the repeat and to keep the spirit of the original whenever you make a change. Few people will discern the difference between the original design and the repeat if the changes are done artistically. Usually a design will look even better in repeat than it did originally because more thought and organization have been put into the finished work.

Some of the changes on an original design that may be required for the repeat are adding or eliminating motifs, making a motif larger or smaller, moving motifs closer together or farther apart, or combining two motifs at the repeat line. By making these changes, the repeat artist is creating a smoothly flowing effect at the repeat line, which is where the repetition of the pattern occurs in the printing.

A roller is a copper cylinder with a circumference of about 15 inches to 18 inches for apparel designs and up to 36 inches for home-furnishing designs. When a design is to be roller printed (most apparel designs), it must be planned so that the vertical repeat fits exactly into the circumference of the printing roller. *Any measurement that fits exactly into the repeat size may be used.* This means, for instance, that if you are asked to put a design into an 18-inch repeat, and the motifs are small and do not require that much space for a good layout, you can put the design into a 9-inch repeat that will be engraved twice on the circumference of the 18-inch roller, a 6-inch repeat that will be engraved three times on the roller, or if the design is even smaller, it might fit a 4½-inch repeat that will be engraved four times on the roller. A very tiny design might only require a 2-inch repeat that would be engraved nine times on the roller and meet at 18 inches as the fabric is printed. The finished fabric will show the same design repeated over and over down the length of the cloth, with a unit reappearing every 6, 9, or 18 inches or whatever other repeat size was used. A plain striped fabric will show nothing but a continuous stripe running the length of the cloth.

The design must also fit the length of the roller, which is the width of the cloth and can be from 36 inches to 60 inches. This measurement can be called the horizontal, width, or side repeat. For simplicity in this chapter, I will use the term side repeat. All repeats have a vertical and side repeat. When you are given a repeat to do, you will always be told the vertical repeat size of the roller or screen. Sometimes the side repeat size is also given, as in home-furnishing designs. When no side repeat size is specified, you can make the side repeat narrower or wider, to fit the demands of the design. This flexibility is an advantage, as a wider side repeat allows more space, if needed, for a balanced arrangement of motifs in the layout. The vertical repeat always has to remain within the confines of the given repeat size. Of course, a small repeat means less to paint, since you only have to paint one full unit of the design in repeat. But do not try to save time by compressing the motifs in the design into a repeat size that is too small. Deciding on the correct repeat size requires careful examination of the design for the variety of motifs, distribution of colors, and so on. Make sure the repeat size you choose allows enough space to include everything.

Half-drop and square repeats

There are two basic kinds of repeats: a half-drop and a square. For purposes of comparison, Figures 7-1a and 7-1b illustrate the same paisley motif in the two repeats.

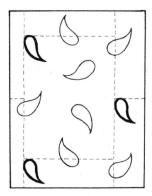

FIGURE 7-1a: A paisley motif laid out in a half-drop repeat. The dark motifs indicate the half-drop.

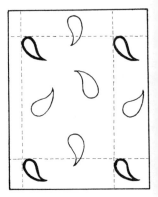

FIGURE 7-1b: The same motif laid out in a square repeat. The dark motifs indicate the square.

A square repeat is laid out in the same arrangement as squares of tile on the floor: Each side of tile matches the side of the next tile to create a continuous pattern (see Figure 7-2b). This is fairly easy to visualize, but the term *square repeat* is somewhat misleading. A square repeat is not necessarily equal in length and width: Any rectangular or box-shaped side repeat is considered a square repeat.

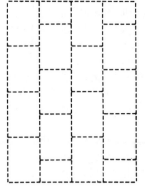

FIGURE 7-2a: The dotted lines show a layout of a continuous half-drop repeat.

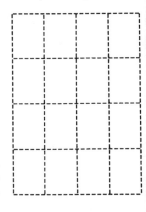

FIGURE 7-2b: The dotted lines show a layout of a continuous square repeat.

A half-drop repeat is laid out on the same basic principle as the square repeat, except that you simply drop the side repeat at exactly half of the vertical repeat size (see Figure 7-2a). On an 18-inch repeat, the half-drop is at 9 inches; on a 9-inch repeat, the half-drop is at 4½ inches; and on a 6-inch repeat, the half-drop is at 3 inches, and so on.

The half-drop is sometimes called the brick layout because it resembles the way in which bricks are laid out, as shown in Figure 7-2a. Figure 7-3 shows a wallpaper printed in a half-drop repeat, and Figure 7-4 shows a fabric printed in a square repeat.

FIGURE 7-3:   A wallpaper designed in a set layout with a half-drop repeat. (Designed by Joan Nelsen)

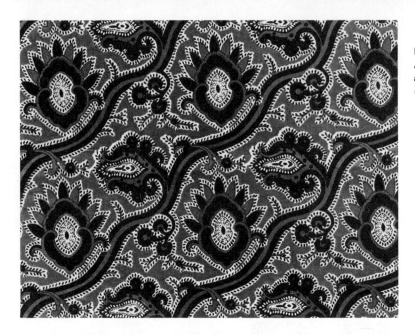

FIGURE 7-4:
A fabric with a flowing layout in a square repeat.
(*Souleiado at Pierre Deux*)

Step-by-step guide for a half-drop repeat

This guide can be used for *all types of designs* and on *all sizes of repeats*, for home furnishings as well as apparel. I have geared the guide to a design in a tossed, all-over layout (since that is usually most difficult for students), and the design is in an 18-inch half-drop repeat, which is a standard size for apparel designs.

The vertical repeat line is worked out first; remember, any measurement that can be divided equally into the given repeat size can be used.

1. **Study the design to decide the vertical repeat size into which it will fit.**

To do this, pick out a motif in the upper left-hand corner of the design. Place your ruler at the top of this motif, as in Figure 7-5a, and glance down to 18 inches. Envision that same motif starting again at that point. Now study the other motifs in the design. Does the design need the full 18 inches to fit in all the motifs and color variations? Glance down to 9 inches on the ruler: Would that work? Or would 6 inches be large enough?

Here is where careful judgment must be used. A small repeat size will obviously save you some work, but don't be too stingy or you will be squeezing the design into a repeat size that is too small, one that does not allow enough space for a good layout. (Keep in mind the possibility of making a wide repeat to provide more space.) When you have determined the proper repeat size for the design, you are ready for step 2.

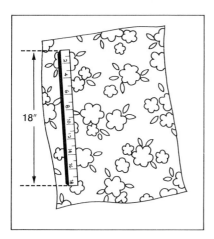

FIGURE 7-5a:
Measuring the design to
determine the repeat size.

2. Rule out two pieces of tracing paper with the vertical repeat measurement.

Square off two pieces of tracing paper (number them 1 and 2) with your triangle and measure both of them to the exact size of the repeat, as in Figures 7-5b and 7-5c. Put in the half-drop line on the right side of both tracings, at exactly half of the vertical repeat size (at 9 inches for an 18-inch repeat, 4½ inches for a 9-inch repeat, 3 inches for a 6-inch repeat, etc.). Write *Top* on the top of all tracings immediately. As the work progresses, the tracings are turned over and around many times and it is very easy to get top and bottom confused. Top clearly written, will eliminate the confusion.

FIGURE 7-5b: Tracing no. 1 ruled with the exact vertical repeat measurement and half-drop line.

FIGURE 7-5c: Tracing no. 2 Duplicate of tracing no. 1.

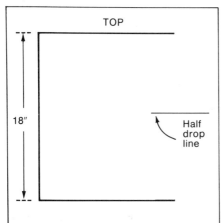

Tracing No. 1

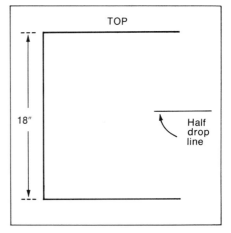

Tracing No. 2

TOP

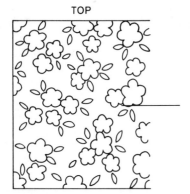

Tracing No. 1

FIGURE 7-5d:
Tracing no. 1 with complete
design traced on it.

On most home-furnishing designs, both the vertical and the side repeat size will be given to you. In these cases, measure and draw in the side repeat line when you reach this point in the step-by-step guide; and when you come to step 6, ignore the directions given since the side repeat line is already drawn.

3. **Trace the complete design on tracing 1 (as in Figure 7-5d).**

4. **Trace only the top and left side of the design on tracing 2 (as in Figure 7-5e).**

5. **Butt the top repeat line of tracing 2 against the bottom repeat line of tracing 1 (as in Figure 7-5f).**

TOP

Tracing No. 2

FIGURE 7-5e:
Tracing no. 2 with the top and left
side of the design traced on it.

TOP

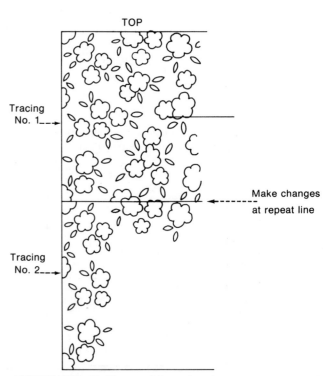

Tracing
No. 1

Make changes
at repeat line

Tracing
No. 2

FIGURE 7-5f: Tracing no. 2 butted against the bottom repeat line of tracing no. 1.

With the two tracings in position as in Figure 7-5f, you can easily see how the design looks at the repeat line. You now make the necessary changes and adjustments by adding, eliminating, moving, or combining motifs to make a smooth flow at the repeat line. Any changes or additions made on one tracing must be made on the other tracing. Here are some problems you may encounter in making these adjustments:

a. The original design is smaller in overall size than the size of the repeat. For example, only 6 inches of the original design have been painted, but the motifs require a 9-inch repeat. This means 3 inches of design have to be filled in on the tracing paper to complete the repeat. Make sure that when you fill in the 3 inches, the flow of all the motifs in the design is balanced. Do not try to either cram a lot of little motifs together to fill in the space or squeeze in a motif that is too large for the space. In order to achieve an overall balance as you fill out the extra amount of design, you may have to change the position of some or even all of the motifs.

When a design has to be extended only an inch or two, it is possible to do the repeat without adding new motifs simply by slightly enlarging all the motifs in the design (a photostat is convenient when the design is too complicated to enlarge by eye). However, do not do this if the enlargement of the motifs significantly changes the scale of the design.

b. The original design is larger than the repeat size. For example, the original design is 24 inches and the repeat is 18 inches. In this case, you must eliminate and/or combine motifs at the repeat line. When these changes are made, be sure the area does not look too crowded or too sparse. This can be checked by looking at the layout from a distance or in a mirror in order to see it in a different perspective. Another way of checking the layout is to make a separate tracing of one particular motif, eliminating all the other elements in the design. This tracing will tell you at a glance whether the distribution of that motif balances in the layout. Separate tracings can then be made of other motifs to see if they are distributed evenly.

c. Look carefully at the spaces formed by the background. Make sure they balance. If there is a conspicuous hole in the background, fill it either by moving the surrounding motifs or by adding other motifs. This may create new spaces in the background and require changing the position of some of the other motifs to obtain a balanced layout.

If a vertical, horizontal, or diagonal channel is being formed in the background that does not appear elsewhere in the design, a correction must be made. Always keep an eye on the overall layout. Moving one motif can sometimes mean having to move many others in order to balance the spaces. Sometimes it is possible simply to take elements of motifs that already appear in the design, such as a leaf or small flower, and fill in an open spot. Make sure any addition is compatible to the surrounding area. Also check to see if the motifs are forming a line that does not appear elsewhere in the design. If so, break up the line by redistributing some of the motifs. Also remember to distribute the motifs two ways if the design requires it. (See Chapter 5 for two-way layout.)

Again let me emphasize that *when you make any change or addition on one tracing, be sure to make the same change on the other tracing* so that the tracings will match as you work back and forth between them.

6. You are now ready to work out the side measurement of the half-drop repeat.

Wallpaper, sheets, pillowcases, and some drapery repeats require a specific side measurement. However, on most apparel designs and some home-furnishing designs, the repeat artist can decide the width of the repeat; on these designs, the number of times the pattern is repeated across the width of the fabric (from selvage to selvage) does not matter. This gives the artist the option of making the repeat wider or narrower as required to accommodate the motifs. If the design can be worked into a narrow repeat, it has the advantage of being a smaller area to paint.

In a repeat where a specific side measurement is required, simply mark the measurement on both tracings and proceed as described below in step c. In cases where the side measure is left to the discretion of the repeat artist, use the following procedure:

    a. Place the top of tracing 2 at the half-drop line of tracing 1 (Figure 7-5g). Decide in what measurement (narrower or wider) the lower part of the half-drop fits.

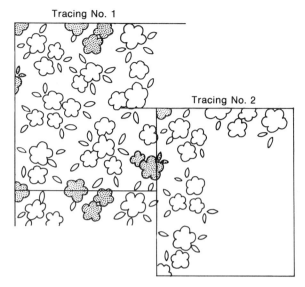

FIGURE 7-5g:
The top of tracing no. 2 placed at the lower half-drop line of tracing no. 1. The dark flowers show changes that had to be made at the vertical repeat line and the lower half-drop line. All changes must be made at all corresponding repeat lines as shown by the dark motifs.

Tracing No. 1

Tracing No. 2

b. Move the bottom of tracing 2 to the upper part of the half-drop line (Figure 7-5h) and decide at what point the upper part of the half-drop fits. There is a possibility that one of the halves will require more space in which to fit the motifs. In this case, the other half must be adjusted and moved to fit in that measurement. When you have determined the measurement that will accommodate both parts of the half-drop, draw in the side repeat line.

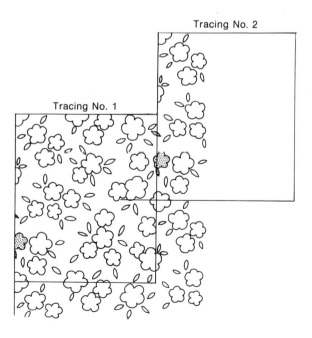

Tracing No. 2

Tracing No. 1

FIGURE 7-5h:
Tracing no. 2 moved to the upper half-drop line. Dark motifs indicate changes that had to be made.

c. You are now ready to rearrange the motifs at the half-drop repeat lines. Return tracing 2 to the lower half-drop line on tracing 1, as in Figure 7-5g, and add, eliminate, or move motifs to make the design flow smoothly. (Any changes or additions that are made on one tracing must be made on the other tracing so that the two always match.)

d. Return tracing 2 to the upper part of the half-drop line on tracing 1, as in Figure 7-5h. Rearrange the motifs as you did on the bottom half-drop line, making sure that the motifs flow smoothly at the line where the two halves meet.

e. Do not be afraid to place a motif on top of the repeat line that is drawn on the tracing paper because you think that all the motifs have to be enclosed within the rigid outlines of the repeat line. On the contrary, placing the motifs in a tossed layout on the repeat line prevents the creation of an obvious empty space that frames the repeat and also helps to create a layout with a continuous flow. If a motif is on the repeat line on the tracing paper, half of it will appear in one unit of repeat on the fabric and the other half of it will appear in the next unit.

f. When you have completed the vertical and horizontal repeats, drawn neatly on tracing 1 (if this is too messy, redraw the finished repeat on clean tracing paper), square off the repeat; it is now ready to be prepared for painting. The artist is responsible for painting one full unit of the repeat plus small overlaps on the bottom and right side, as illustrated in Figure 7-5i.

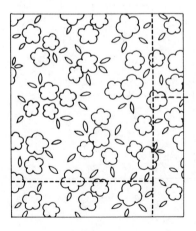

FIGURE 7-5i:
The completed tracing of the half-drop repeat, with small overlaps on the bottom and right sides, ready to prepare for painting. This illustrates the area of the repeat that has to be painted.

Step-by-step guide for a square repeat

Follow steps 1 through 5 as described in the previous section (refer to Figures 7-5a through 7-5f); delete all half-drop lines and proceed as follows:

You are now ready to work out the side measurement of the square repeat.

a. Place tracing 2 next to tracing 1 so the top lines of both tracings line up (Figure 7-6a). Decide in what width measurement (narrower or wider) the motifs at the side repeat line will fit. Then draw in the side repeat line on both tracings.

b. You are now ready to rearrange the motifs at the side repeat line by eliminating, adding, moving, or combining motifs to make the design flow smoothly, as shown in Figure 7-6b.

c. Tracing 2 can now be moved down to complete the square repeat. This is shown on the lower right-hand section of Figure 7-6b.

d. When you have completed the square repeat, drawn neatly on tracing 1 (if this is too messy, redraw the finished repeat on clean tracing paper), square off the repeat; it is now ready to be prepared for painting. The artist is responsible for painting one full unit of the repeat plus small overlaps on the bottom and right side.

Tracing No. 1   Tracing No. 2

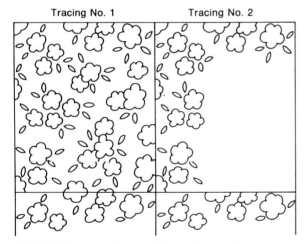

FIGURE 7-6a: Tracing no. 2 in position next to tracing no. 1 ready for the side repeat line to be determined.

FIGURE 7-6b:
The completed square repeat. Dark motifs indicate changes that had to be made at the side repeat line. This illustrates the area of the repeat that has to be painted.

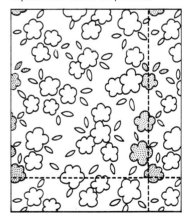

Color distribution

A color-distribution layout is needed for most designs before the painting of the repeat can begin. Place a clean sheet of tracing paper on top of the repeat. Use colored pencils, crayons, or just letters — Y for yellow, B for blue, R for red — to indicate the different colors.

The distribution of the colors in the repeat should closely resemble the original design unless a color change has been ordered; however, colors can be moved around wherever necessary to balance them in the layout. Often one color will be overrepresented at the repeat line as a result of the redistribution of the motifs. To correct this, respot the color; the surrounding colors often have to be changed as well.

Separate tracings can be made of each color to double check that the color spotting balances in the overall layout and especially at the repeat lines. When you are satisfied that the color distribution is correct, mix the colors. Make sure to mix enough of all the colors to finish painting the repeat and have some left over for touch-ups.

Painting the repeat on opaque paper

When the repeat is to be painted on opaque paper, use one of the following two methods to transfer the repeat from the tracing paper to the drawing paper.

The first method is to "back" one full unit of the repeat tracing in pencil, preparatory to rubbing it down on the drawing paper. (This technique is described in Chapter 5.) Back only one unit; it is best to rub down the same unit when you move the tracing to the half-drop or square repeat lines. This is also a good way to check on the correctness of the repeat. If the rubdown does not match up at all the repeat lines, you can identify the error and make the correction on the tracing before you start painting.

The second method of transferring the repeat is to trace it on the drawing paper with Saral transfer paper as described in Chapter 2. If a ground is required, it must, of course, be painted before the repeat is transferred. The next step is to measure out the repeat lines on the drawing paper. Do not put heavy pencil marks on the drawing paper unless they will eventually be covered with opaque paint or the drawing paper permits easy erasures. Register marks are sufficient.

Position the tracing on the drawing paper, matching the repeat lines or register marks exactly. Tape the tracing down and rub down or trace (using transfer paper) the repeat on the drawing paper. Next, move the tracing to the vertical repeat line, match up the repeat lines, and rub down or trace a small overlap of the repeat. Move the tracing to the right, to the lower part of the half-drop or the square, and match up the repeat lines. Rub down or trace the overlap. Finally, move the tracing to the upper part of the half-drop and rub down or trace that section. Square off the completed repeat with a triangle and you are ready to start painting.

Keep the original design in clear view as you paint. The tracing tells you where to paint but doesn't show the technique or the subtleties of painting the motifs. Only the original design, whether it was created by you or someone else, can show you this. Look at the original frequently as you paint to make sure that the flowers are not becoming too large or the leaves too heavy. Remember, the customer has bought a design and expects the repeat to look as much like it as possible, even though changes have been made.

When the repeat does not require too many changes from the original design, and a large portion of the original matches the repeat exactly in layout and color spotting, it may be possible to use part of the original in the repeat. Carefully cut out the usable section with an Exacto knife and paste or tape it on a fresh piece of matching drawing paper. Use the same procedure as above: Put register marks on the drawing paper and rub down or trace the remainder of the repeat. By pasting up a portion of the design in this fashion, a lot of time can be saved in doing the repeat.

Painting the repeat on waxed rice paper

When the repeat is to be painted on waxed rice paper, there are a few special instructions to follow. Because it is not easy to make erasures on waxed rice paper, you should not use a pencil to rub down or trace. It is best to work out the full repeat on tracing paper with the overlaps on the bottom and right sides as in Figure 7-5i. The tracing should be clear and accurate. Double-check the repeat lines before starting to paint.

When this is done, place the sheet of waxed rice paper (which is transparent) on top of the tracing, and proceed to paint the repeat. Be sure it is taped or tacked down so it does not slip while you are painting. Finish the repeat, following the same procedure as described for painting on opaque paper.

Some designers prefer to fill in one color on the entire repeat wherever it appears and then go on to the next color. Others prefer completing all the colors in one section of the design and then going on to paint the next area. Each person should work in the manner most comfortable for her or him. It is helpful sometimes to use one brush for each color.

When the painting of the repeat is completed, and all pencil lines are erased, a repeat is squared off with a triangle, cut out, and mounted. It is then sent to the mill for the next step in printing the fabric.

Stripe repeat

At the beginning of this chapter I noted that a plain stripe pattern, when printed, appears as a continuous stripe running the length of the fabric. This kind of simple stripe requires only a side repeat, but most stripes are designed with many motifs and thus require both a vertical and side repeat. When doing a stripe repeat, follow the step-by-step repeat guide and the special instructions listed below. Although a tossed design was used to illustrate the guide, the formula was devised to work on all types of designs.

As you master repeats, you may discover shortcuts or learn other ways to do them. Until then, I recommend carefully following the steps outlined in this chapter.

Special instructions for a stripe repeat

1. A stripe repeat has a vertical and side repeat that must be worked out the same way as a tossed repeat (follow the step-by-step guide).
2. Always make a right angle (square off) on the paper with a triangle when you start a stripe layout. This gives you a horizontal line and a vertical line from which to measure the width of each stripe.
3. Measure the width of each stripe, even if the design calls for the motifs in the stripe to be loosely laid out, that is, not entirely confined within the rigid outlines of the stripe.
4. Measure the position of the *motifs* in each stripe so that they divide equally into the repeat size (see Figures 7-7 and 7-8).
5. Measure the *spaces* between the motifs in each stripe to be certain that they also divide equally into the repeat size.
6. The side repeat on a stripe design can be either a half-drop (Figure 7-8) or a square (Figure 7-7).
7. All the motifs in each stripe in the design, even minor ones, must be put into repeat, so that the design can be printed in a continuous flow.

FIGURE 7-7:
A two-way stripe for
apparel wear in a square
repeat.
(©Carol Joyce)

FIGURE 7-8:
A one-way home furnishing stripe
in a half-drop repeat.
(*Brunschwig & Fils, Inc.*)

Border repeat

Special instructions for a border repeat

1. The border on a design is printed along the edge or selvage of the fabric; therefore, the design is turned on its side when the repeat is made, as in Figure 7-9.
2. The border is put into a vertical repeat the same way as a stripe.
3. The pattern that appears above the border is called the field.
4. The field is put into either a half-drop (Figure 7-10a) or a square repeat (Figure 7-10b), with both a vertical and side repeat.
5. One full unit of the field painted in repeat is enough to indicate to the printer that the remainder of the field continues in that same repeat across the width of the fabric (Figure 7-9).

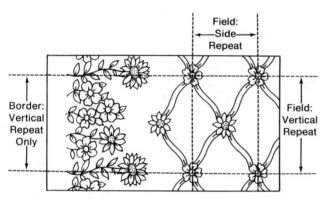

FIGURE 7-9:
The correct position for a border design when working on the repeat. The dotted lines show the border and field repeat lines.

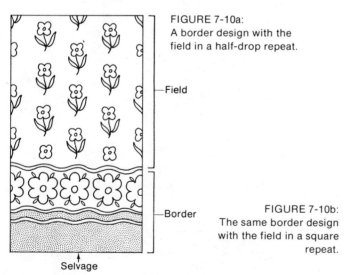

FIGURE 7-10a:
A border design with the field in a half-drop repeat.

FIGURE 7-10b:
The same border design with the field in a square repeat.

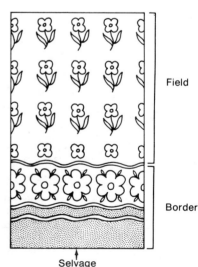

Border design with a flip repeat

Another variation of a border design is illustrated in Figure 7-11, which shows a pattern with a border along both edges or selvages of the design. As the illustration shows, the design, when folded in half, creates an exact mirror image. This is called a flip or flop repeat: Half of the design is painted in repeat and then it is flipped (or flopped) in the printing process to complete the design across the width of the fabric.

Sometimes, a pattern will require only a quarter of the repeat to be painted, because all four quarters are exactly the same, as shown in Figure 7-13. Flip repeats are usually found on designs for handkerchiefs, scarves, and towels as well as piece goods.

If you have a flip repeat in which the center motif is *not* a mirror image, paint half the design (or one quarter, as in Figure 7-12) in repeat plus the entire center motif. The rest of the design will be flipped in the printing process.

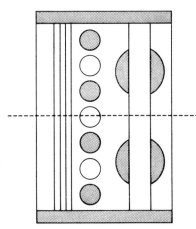

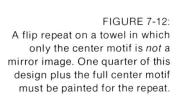

FIGURE 7-12: A flip repeat on a towel in which only the center motif is *not* a mirror image. One quarter of this design plus the full center motif must be painted for the repeat.

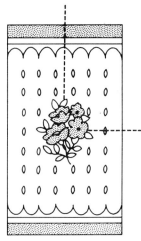

FIGURE 7-11: A design for a towel that creates a mirror image when folded in half. Only half of the design has to be painted for the repeat, as indicated by the dotted line. This is called a flip repeat. Tho othor half ic flippod in tho printing process.

FIGURE 7-13: A scarf design in which all four quarters are the same. Only one quarter has to be painted for this flip repeat.

Chapter eight

Special design techniques

This chapter will describe some techniques with which you can create special effects on your designs. The first is a simple transfer method for adding a batik effect to an otherwise completed design.

Batik

There are several ways of creating a batik effect on paper. The advantage of the following method is that you can apply the batik on top of any design painted in dye colors, often greatly enhancing it.

Batik is an ancient wax resist method of printing designs on fabric. A design is applied in wax to the surface of the fabric, the fabric is then dipped into dye, and the areas that have been waxed resist penetration by that color. The wax is then removed. Additional designs can then be applied in wax to obtain different patterns and colors.

A unique characteristic of batik is the crackle effect that

is caused when the wax cracks and dye penetrates through the cracks to the fabric. However, we are not concerned here with batiking on fabric. The textile designer must imitate this crackle effect on paper, so that when the design is printed commercially, the fabric will have this batik look (shown in Figure 8-1).

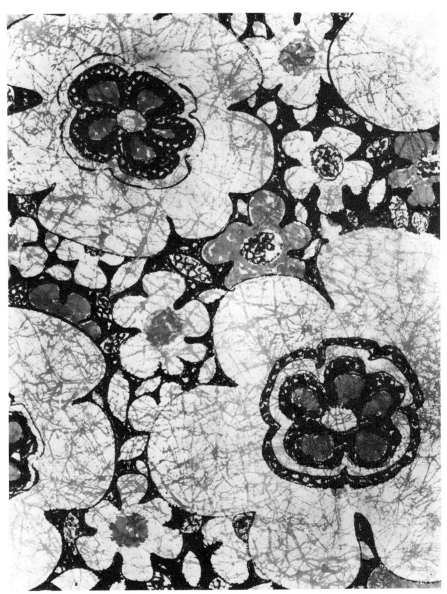

FIGURE 8-1: A floral design painted in dyes with a batik effect laid on top of it. (©Carol Joyce)

Supplies for batiking

1. A completed design painted in dyes, preferably on tweed weave, Bristol, or other slightly porous paper, although designs on waxed rice paper can also be batiked. The design should be of the type that lends itself to the batik look: exotic floral, Oriental, African, or similar ethnic motifs.
2. A piece of waxed rice paper (can be imperfect).
3. Dyes. Sepia is a good neutral batik color that looks well on most designs. Two batik colors can be used on a design if needed.
4. A No. 7 or No. 8 brush or a small ground brush.
5. A roll of paper towels.
6. Non Crawl and/or liquid soap.
7. Test paper — can be an old design or scrap paper of the same kind to be used for the batik.
8. Scrap paper to spread under the work to avoid mess. (Do not use newspaper for this purpose as the print may stain your design.)

Procedure

1. Take a piece of waxed rice paper about five or six inches square. Crush it slowly, inch by inch, in your hand. Crush it firmly but gently. Try not to tear it but don't worry if you make a small rip. The crushed wax on the paper creates the cracks through which the dye will penetrate onto the design. After you have crushed the paper, flatten and smooth it out. Hold it up to the light and you will see the cracks that will form the batik pattern when the dye is pressed through it.
2. Mix a few drops of Non Crawl or liquid soap in the dye to be used for the batik color. (Some designers prefer to apply the Non Crawl or soap directly to the crackle paper.) The use of either of these media helps to push the dye through the cracks; try both and decide which works better for you.
3. Next, with your brush apply a few strokes of dye on the crackle paper, leaving the edges unpainted so the paper can be handled. Lay the crackle paper, *dye side up*, on the test paper, and with a crushed paper towel, press down, stroke, and push the dye through the cracks to the test paper underneath.
4. Lift up the crackle paper and see how the batik effect has transferred onto the test paper. If the crackle is not

coming through, press down again with the paper towel. Then try a little more Non Crawl. If it still does not transfer, it probably means the transfer paper is not cracked enough. Start over and crush another piece of waxed rice paper more vigorously. If too much color is being transferred through the crackle paper, you have used either too much dye or too much Non Crawl.

5. When the batik effect looks right on the test paper, immediately place the crackle paper on top of the design to be batiked, *dye side up*, and press the batik through with the paper towel. Move the crackle paper to a new area on the design and after pressing it down, lift it up to check how the batik effect looks. Add more color on the crackle paper when needed. When more color is added, it is a good idea to test the crackle effect on scrap paper before transferring it to the design. If the crackle paper is worn, throw it away and crush a new one.

6. By substituting bleach for dye, the same method of batiking may be used to create a white batik on a design. This is especially helpful in areas where the design looks too heavy and dark. The combination of dark and light batik effect works very well on some designs. Non Crawl must be used with the bleach.

By using a small piece of crackle paper, you get maximum control over the batiking process. You are able to move the crackle paper easily from area to area, checking the results as you work. You can add more batik, if needed, by pressing the crackle paper on an area two or three times.

It is also possible to use a large piece of crushed wax rice paper that is placed over the entire design. Flatten out the crushed paper, place it on a test paper, and apply the Non Crawl and dye with a large ground brush. Press the batik through to the test paper with paper towels. When you determine that the large crackle paper on the test paper looks right, place the crackle paper over your design and transfer the batik effect by pressing down with long strokes on the paper towels. Lift up the crackle paper occasionally to check how the batik looks on the design. Add more color, if needed, and press down harder on areas where the batik is too light.

Incidentally, it is possible to reverse the process by starting with a batik background and painting the design on top of it. To do this, apply the crushed wax paper directly to a fresh piece of drawing paper and press the dye through it to create a batik background ready for design.

Bleach HOW TO DESIGN WITH BLEACH
ON A DYED BACKGROUND

This technique is used on a design with a dyed background. It is an alternative to painting the background around the motifs (blotching). The bleach makes it possible to design by removing areas of color from a dyed ground and either applying new color to the areas or leaving them white. This technique is particularly effective when light or bright colors have to be used on darker grounds (for an example see Color Plate 1).

Procedure

1. Mix the dye and paint the ground. (See Chapter 6 for instructions on painting grounds.) Save the leftover dye for touch-ups.

2. If the ground is on opaque paper, transfer the design to it either by the rubdown method (Chapter 5) or the transfer-paper method (Chapter 2). When the ground is on waxed rice paper, the design should be clearly drawn on tracing paper first. The waxed paper ground is then taped on top of the tracing and is ready for painting. Dark-colored grounds may require the use of a light box.

3. If there are any fine-line outlines in the design draw them with waterproof ink or waterproof magic marker.

4. Decide on the color distribution in the design (see Chapter 6) so you can determine which motifs to bleach out. On motifs where the dye colors can be painted right over the background color, it is not necessary to bleach them out. For example, orange, red, or green can usually be put on a yellow ground without changing the top colors in any significant way. Most colors painted on a beige ground will be slightly muted but still will look fine. Test colors first, if you are uncertain whether to bleach an area or not.

5. Apply the bleach with an old brush. (Never use a good brush, as the bleach will eat out the hairs.) A toothpick is also handy for applying bleach to small areas; a cotton swab or something similar, for larger areas. It is a good idea to start by applying the bleach in the center of the area you are working on and then push the drops toward the edges of the area, trying not to touch the outlines of the motif or go beyond them with the bleach. However, if the bleach does go over the outline, this area can be touched up with matching color later.

6. Leave the bleach on the motif for a minute or two and then carefully blot it up with a tissue. The bleach should not be kept on too long or it will eat out the surface of the paper. If the area does not look white enough after one application, reapply the bleach for another minute and blot up again. The lighter the ground color is, the faster the bleach will work. Dark grounds may retain a slight residue of color on the bleached areas. This should present no problem, as the color you put over it will cover it. Of course, if you want the area to remain pure white, try another coat of bleach and/or paint over it with pro-white.

7. Let the bleached areas dry well before reapplying color or the new color will be eaten out by the residue of bleach on the paper.

OTHER BLEACH TECHNIQUES

Bleach can be used on designs painted in dyes to obtain different special effects. Some of these are described and shown in Figures 8-2 and 8-3. Use your imagination to create other effects with bleach.

FIGURE 8-2: In this illustration, the dyed background was painted first on waxed paper. Second, the outlines of the bird were drawn with waterproof ink. Finally, the white feather effect on the bird was achieved by drawing with a toothpick dipped into bleach.

FIGURE 8-3:   The waves on this design were painted in dyes. The white lines on the waves were made with a very fine pen point dipped into bleach.

Flower shading

Because flowers are the most frequently used motifs in textile design, the ability to draw and shade flowers is very important for the designer (see Color Plates 7 and 11). There are three ways to shade flowers.

Figure 8-4 shows a flower that is shaded by using three related colors to create a three-dimensional look. To achieve such a look, use the following method:

FIGURE 8-4:
A flower in which three related colors are used to create a three-dimensional look.

1. Mix three related colors in either gouache or dye: one light, one medium, and one dark. These can be either three tones of the same color — such as dark blue, medium blue, and light blue — or they can be colors that are related but not the same — such as red, orange, and yellow.

2. Start by applying paint to the petal nearest the center of the flower. The petal can be entirely covered or the ground color can be allowed to show through. When applying paint, be certain to follow the contour of the petal as this is the natural flow of the shading effect.

3. Start with the lightest color and follow with the medium color. The last color applied is the darkest. Small highlights of color or white can be added to enhance the three-dimensional effect.

Figure 8-5 shows a flower shaded by using one color applied on the paper and then shaded from dark to light to create an ombre effect. Use the following technique:

1. Work on each petal separately. Paint a shape with the color, starting at the inside of the petal. As you apply the paint, always follow the contour of the petal.
2. Quickly clean the brush (or use a second one) and with a moist brush begin shading the color, dark to light, toward the outer edge of the petal. Smooth out the shading.
3. To make the flower look more realistic, one side can be shaded more heavily than the other. Highlights of the full-strength color or white can be added for emphasis. Once you have mastered this simple way of shading, you can create your own variations of it on leaves and other motifs. A good way to practice is to copy flowers from printed fabrics. Trace the motifs, and using the above methods as a guide, paint them. This will help you develop an important skill.

Figure 8-6 shows another, very simple way to make a flower look three dimensional. This is done by simply using one flat color to shape the flower without shading. Always follow the contour of the petal when you apply the paint. Dye, gouache, or tempera can be used.

FIGURE 8-5: A flower using one color shaded from dark to light.

FIGURE 8-6: A three-dimensional look achieved by painting with one flat color.

Stipple

Stipple is a method of using small dots instead of lines or solid areas for shading motifs and backgrounds. Tools that can be used to create stipple effects are pen and ink, brush, Magic Marker, technical ink pen, and a special dotting pen (see Chapter 2, Materials and Supplies). Depending on the design, gouache, dye, colored pencil, and crayon can also be used to make the stipple dots.

Darker shading is achieved by placing the dots closer together. The gradual dispersing of the dots farther and farther apart will create a dark-to-light shaded effect. Stippling is shown on a flower in Figure 8-7 and in a background in Figure 8-8.

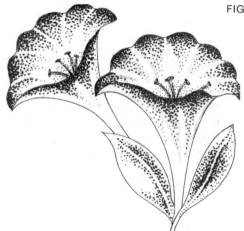

FIGURE 8-7:   A flower shaded with a stipple technique.

FIGURE 8-8:   A floral pattern with a stipple dot in the background. (*Brunschwig & Fils, Inc.*)

Sponge This is a technique to create a textured effect by using a sponge to daub paint on the design. Different sponges can be used according to the needs of the design. A fine-textured sponge can be purchased at cosmetic counters. Household sponges will give a coarser effect.

The sponge itself can be cut into a shape such as a leaf and used directly on the design, as in Figure 8-9. The sponge technique can also be used to form textured background effects.

The method is as follows: Apply the paint to the sponge with a brush or dip the bottom of the sponge directly into the paint. Test the sponge on scrap paper to make certain the paint does not blob. The final test on the scrap paper should result in a suitable texture for your design. The texture effect will be heavier or lighter depending on the pressure you put on the sponge.

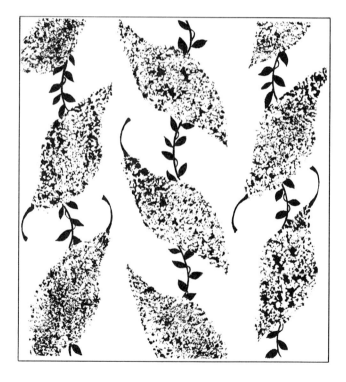

FIGURE 8-9:   The textured effect on this design was made by a sponge cut into a leaf shape.

Spatter

The spatter technique uses a toothbrush and spoon to create shaded color effects that resemble those made by an airbrush. The spatter is similar to the stipple effect but can produce finer shading more quickly. Spatter can be used to shade flowers and other motifs (Figure 8-10) or for textured effects in backgrounds (Figure 8-11). A spatter is often used to create plaids (Figure 8-12) and stripes when a woven look is desired.

FIGURE 8-10:   A design done with a spatter technique to achieve a shaded effect on the motifs.
(*Clarence House Imports, Ltd.*)

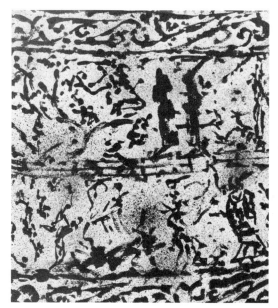

FIGURE 8-11:   A design in which spatter is used to
create a textured background.
(©Carol Joyce)

FIGURE 8-12:   A plaid in which areas were masked
off and spatter applied to create a woven effect.
(©Carol Joyce)

Step-by-step guide to spattering

1. Mask off any areas on the design *not* to be spattered. This can be done with masking tape or Friskit or by cutting a stencil and weighting the edges down with coins or a touch of double-faced tape. Masking materials are lifted off when the spatter is finished. Other areas can then be masked off if a second color is needed.

2. Mix the color desired for the spatter in a small container, using either gouache or dye paints.

3. Hold the toothbrush — *bristle side up* — in your left hand (right hand if you are left-handed) between your thumb and index finger. Get a firm grip on the handle close to the bristles.

4. Stand up over the design for maximum leverage as you spatter. Apply a brushful of paint to the toothbrush.

5. Hold the toothbrush, *bristle side up*, and point it downward over the design to be spattered. Hold the spoon in the other hand between the thumb and index finger. The inside of the bowl of the spoon should be tilted toward you, *facing down* over the bristles at about a 45-degree angle.

6. Begin the spatter by making quick, short strokes with the lower edge of the spoon, moving up the length of the bristles, *always toward you*. Do not stroke away from yourself, as the paint will spatter on you instead of the design.

7. Move the brush and spoon, spattering steadily, at an even pace, on each area to be covered. To make a heavier spatter, go over the area as many times as necessary. To lighten an area that has been spattered too heavily, respatter it with white or the ground color. Bleach also can be spattered on dye.

8. Always test the spatter first on scrap paper to make certain that the color intensity is the one you want. The heaviest spray will occur when you first begin the spatter. As you continue to spatter, the spray will become finer. Add more paint on the toothbrush as needed.

Warp

A warp effect on a design emphasizes the vertical threads that can be seen on a woven fabric. These vertical threads are called the *warp* (the horizontal threads are called the *weft*). Two ways to achieve a warp effect on a design are shown below in Figures 8-13 and 8-14.

FIGURE 8-13:
The warp effect on this apparel design is drawn with pen and ink on top of the motifs.
(©Carol Joyce)

FIGURE 8-14: A home furnishing pattern in which paints were used to create the warp effect. (*Boussac of France, Inc.*)

Stitching and embroidery

A design can be painted entirely of embroidery stitches (Figure 8-15), or stitches can be used on top and around the edges of the motifs to make them appear to be sewn onto the background, creating an applique look (Figure 8-16). Such effects, done with a small brush, felt-tip pens, or pen and ink, are very effective in achieving a patchwork, folk art, or ethnic look.

An embroidery book will give you many ideas for stitches such as those shown in Figure 8-17.

FIGURE 8-15: A folk art border design painted entirely of
bright-colored stitches on a black background. (©Carol Joyce)

FIGURE 8-16:
An applique design done in a
diamond layout. Stitching is
used in and around all the motifs
including the ribbon that forms the
plaid.
(©Carol Joyce)

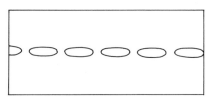

(a) Running stitch

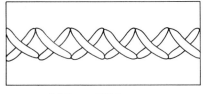

(b) Cross Stitch

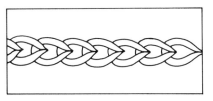

(c) Chain stitch

FIGURE 8-17:
Examples of embroidery stitches
(enlarged) that can be used on designs.

Dry brush

Dry brush is a technique used to paint a shaded effect with a brush stroke. Dip the brush into the paint (which should be a thick, creamy consistency) and stroke it back and forth on scrap paper until enough of the paint is removed, so that the paper shows through when a stroke is made. Figure 8-18 shows a design with leaves and stems done with dry brush.

FIGURE 8-18: A tossed floral design in which the leaves and stems are done in dry brush technique.
(©Carol Joyce)

Touch-up methods

HOW TO MAKE CORRECTIONS

If a correction has to be made on a gouache or tempera design, you can paint right on top of the mistake. On designs made with dyes, try bleaching out the mistakes. Use a toothpick, old brush, or any other suitable applicator, and keep the bleach within the correction area. (See bleach techniques in this chapter.) If the bleach or gouache correction looks sloppy or does not result in an area clean enough to paint over, follow these instructions:

1. With an Exacto knife or a single-edge razor blade, carefully cut out the area to be corrected.

2. Take a fresh piece of the same kind of paper as the design is painted on. Make sure it is a little larger than the cut-out area. Turn the design over, and on the back of it, apply rubber cement around the edges of the hole. Place the new piece of paper over the cut-out area and paste it down. (On waxed rice paper, use double-faced transparent tape or a touch of any glue that will not show, such as Elmer's, to paste down the edges.) Rubber cement can be used on all opaque drawing papers.

3. Turn the design face up and peel off any excess rubber cement. If the two papers seem thick along the edges where they are glued together, turn the design to the back again. Use the edge of a spoon or knife and rub down the edges of the pasted-up area. This will flatten out and tightly adhere the two edges together and allow the paint to go on smoothly.

4. When this touch-up job is done well, it will give you a fresh, clean area to make the correction on, and it will be virtually undetectable. Corrections should not be pasted on top of a design: This looks sloppy and detracts from the design.

5. Another method of cutting out areas to be corrected is called double-cutting. Take a piece of the same kind of paper a design is painted on and place it underneath the area to be cut out. With an Exacto knife or single-edge razor blade, carefully cut out the area to be corrected, *cutting through both papers at the same time*. This will give you a new piece of paper that is an exact duplicate of the area to be corrected.

   Turn the design over, and on the back side, fit the clean duplicate into the hole in the design. Tape it in place around the edges (using transparent tape on waxed rice paper), and make your correction.

Chapter nine

The printing process

This chapter explains the aspects of printing necessary for designers to know. Books listed in the Bibliography will be helpful to those desiring to pursue this subject further.

Printing processes

There are four basic textile printing machine processes.

ROLLER PRINTING

The design is etched on copper rollers, which are chrome-plated for durability. Each color in the design is etched on a separate roller; therefore a five-color pattern would have five rollers. Color is picked up on each roller from a color trough, and the excess is scraped off by a blade known as the doctor blade. This process leaves color only in the etched area of the roller. As the cloth passes through the printing machine, the rollers rotate, and each successive color in the design is printed on the fabric. (See Figures 9-1 and 9-2.)

FIGURE 9-1:
Roller printing. Each color in the design is engraved on a roller. As the cloth passes through the machine, each roller imparts its respective color and pattern to the fabric.
(*American Textile Manufacturers Institute, Inc.*)

FIGURE 9-2:
A side view of a 5-roller printing machine.

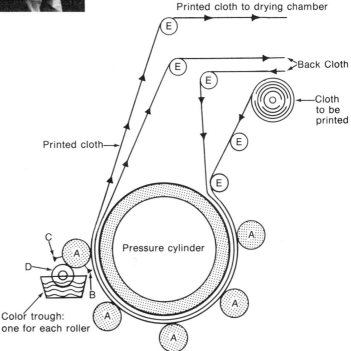

Printed cloth to drying chamber

Back Cloth

Cloth to be printed

Printed cloth→

A—Etched print rollers: one for each color

B—Doctor knife: scrapes excess color off roller

C—Lint doctor: scrapes lint off fabric

D—Color furnisher

E—Guide rollers

Pressure cylinder

Color trough: one for each roller

ROTARY SCREEN PRINTING

A rotary screen is a cylinder of thin flexible metal. A separate rotary screen is needed for each color in the design. The design area to be printed is an open fine mesh in the cylinder. Color is pumped into each cylinder, and as the cylinder rotates, the cloth passes beneath it. A magnetic rod within the cylinder forces color through the mesh onto the cloth. Each color in the design, as in all methods of printing, must be synchronized, so as to print in perfect registration. This method of printing fabric is five or six times faster than flat-bed screen printing. (See Figures 9-3 and 9-4.)

FIGURE 9-3: Rotary screen printing. The newest screen printing process that combines some of the advantages of roller and flat bed screen printing. (*American Textile Manufacturers Institute, Inc.*)

FIGURE 9-4: In rotary screen printing, as the fabric passes under cylindrical screens — one for each color — the pattern is printed. (*Courtesy of Burlington Industries, Inc.*)

FLAT-BED SCREEN PRINTING

In flat-bed screen printing, the screens, which are usually made of strong nylon, are stationary. As the cloth passes beneath the screen, one repeat at a time, color is forced through the screen by a squeegee. The areas not to be printed are coated with a resist substance. The color penetrates the screen only in areas where the nylon has been left porous. A separate screen is used for each color. (See Figures 9-5 and 9-6.)

FIGURE 9-5: Flat-bed screen printing. The design is laid out
on a porous cloth screen, usually made of nylon.
(*American Textile Manufacturers Institute, Inc.*)

FIGURE 9-6: In flat-bed screen printing, color is poured
into the screen and applied to the fabric
by means of a squeegee worked back and forth.
(Courtesy of Burlington Industries, Inc.)

HEAT TRANSFER PRINTING

Heat transfer printing (also known as sublimation printing and dry printing) is a textile printing process that was developed in France in 1966 and came to the United States in 1968. The design is printed first on specially coated paper, instead of directly on the fabric as in other printing methods. The printed paper is then applied to the fabric, and via heat and pressure, the design is transferred to the fabric.

This method of printing is used only on polyester, nylon, and other man-made fabrics, as the dyes that are employed are not suitable for natural fibers. (See Figures 9-7 and 9-8.)

FIGURE 9-7: Heat transfer printing. The design is printed in special ink on paper and then transferred from the paper to the cloth with a combination of heat and pressure. The illustration shows the transfer-printed fabric being separated from exhausted paper. (*Courtesy of Sublistatic Corp. of America*)

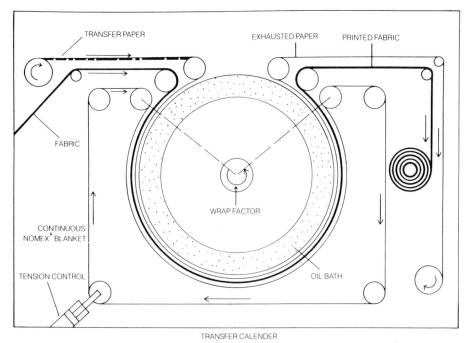

TRANSFER CALENDER

FIGURE 9-8:   A diagram of the heat-transfer printing process.
(*Courtesy of Sublistatic Corp. of America*)

Color printing processes

There are two basic color printing methods.

DIRECT OR APPLICATION PRINTING

In this method, the design motif is printed directly on white or light-colored ground fabrics with a variety of pigment and dye colors.

    Recently pigment colors have been developed that will cover medium to dark ground fabrics with white, light, or bright colors. However, the ground shade will affect the application colors. This is an alternate method to discharge printing, described below.

DISCHARGE OR EXTRACT PRINTING

For discharge printing, medium to dark ground shades are dyed on the fabric first with specially prepared dyestuffs. The top color, which is then printed on the dyed ground, contains a chemical that interacts with the dye. This interaction simultaneously bleaches color from the dyed ground and prints the desired color in its place. Areas can be discharged out and left white.

Since the background color of the fabric is dyed first in discharge printing, bright or light colors or white can be printed on top of medium or dark grounds without the problem of fitting the background blotch around the motifs.

Responsibilities of mill work

The stylist (or someone designated by the stylist) is responsible for the designs being printed satisfactorily on the fabric, which requires going to the printing plant to supervise the printing. A designer is sometimes given this opportunity to learn mill work. A designer who has mill experience can command a higher salary.

The function of the person at the mill is to make sure that the pattern printed on the fabric is clear and esthetically acceptable, and that the colors are correct. Technical problems, such as bowing and warping of the fabric, have to be watched.

The first run of printed fabric is called a strike-off. The strike-offs must be examined and either approved or corrected. The color may have to be brought up (made heavier or brighter) or brought down (made lighter or duller). The printed colors are compared to painted colorways or to color chips that are brought to the mill from the studio. Sometimes the roller or the screen has to be corrected. If so, the pattern is pulled (printing is stopped) until the correction is made.

The first few times a new person goes to the mill to learn printing, she or he is always accompanied by an experienced person. I am always surprised at how fast many of my students become proficient in mill work after only a short on-the-job training period.

Glossary

Acetate   Clear plastic sheets of different weights on which colorways are painted and designs and colors can be tested.

Americana   A design whose motifs derive from American history, either traditional or modern.

Apparel Designs (sometimes called *Fashion*)   A textile design created tor men's, women's, or children's wear.

Application or Direct Printing   A method of printing in which color is printed directly on white or light ground fabric.

Applique   A motif embroidered or sewn on a fabric.

Art Deco   An art movement (1910-1930s) characterized by design that has angular, geometric, and stylized motifs.

Art Nouveau   An art movement (1900-1920), characterized by sensuous, flowing motifs derived from nature.

Backing   To retrace the pencil lines (of a design) on the back of a tracing to prepare it for the rubdown.

Batik   A resist method of decorating fabric in which areas of a design are covered with wax before the fabric is immersed in dye. The waxed areas resist the dye; the wax is removed, revealing the design. The process may be repeated several times with different colors for varying effects.

Bayadere   A design that is laid out in a horizontal stripe.

Block Printing   This is the oldest form of printing, in which motifs are hand printed with wooden, copper, or linoleum blocks.

Blotch   The ground color painted or printed around the motifs in a design.

Botanical   A realistic, well-drawn design consisting of fine-line motifs such as those found in illustrated botanical books.

Bright Pastel   A coloring using tones of color that fall between primary and pastel.

Bristol Paper   A white drawing paper with a slightly textured surface.

Calico   One of the oldest cotton fabrics, originating in Calcutta, India. Calico patterns are typically small floral patterns, sometimes stylized, in a variety of bright colors.

Chintz   Glazed cotton fabric, of Indian origin, often printed with figuratives and large flower designs, used mainly for home decoration.

Color Spotting   A method of determining the balanced distribution of colors in a design by marking each different color on a tracing overlay.

Colorway, Coloring, Color Combination   A section of a design painted to show the pattern in a different color combination.

Conversational   A design with realistic or stylized motifs that suggest a story.

Converter   A company that purchases gray goods and converts them into printed fabric.

Coordinate, Twin, or Companion Pattern   A design created with the same feeling and color as another pattern so that they may be used together.

Country French   Designs that originated in Provence, and derive from eighteenth-century woodblocks. They are often small and neat with borders, and are designed and colored to coordinate with each other.

Croquis   A small sketch or preparatory rendering of a design.

Crow Quill Pen   An artist's penpoint that produces a very fine line.

Decoratives   Home-furnishing designs for drapery, upholstery, wallpaper, and the like.

Discharge or Extract Printing   A method of printing used on medium- to dark-colored ground fabrics to obtain white or colored motifs. The top color contains a chemical that simultaneously bleaches color out of the dyed ground and prints the desired color in its place.

Documentary   A design taken from a decorative historical document.

Domestics   Home-furnishing designs for sheets, pillowcases, towels, and bedspreads.

Dry Brush   A technique for shading motifs, using a brush dipped in paint and then stripped of enough of the paint to allow the paper to show through the brush stroke.

Duplex Printing   A method of printing on both sides of a fabric using the same or different motifs.

Dyes, Concentrated Watercolors   Brilliant, transparent colors that are lightened with water and can be mixed together to create other colors.

Engineer Print   A print that is designed and laid out to the specifications of the pattern from which the garment will be cut.

Field   The area in a border design that is printed above the border across the width of the fabric to the selvage.

Flat-Bed Screen Printing   In this process, the screens, one for each color, remain stationary. As the cloth passes beneath the screen, dye penetrates the screen and prints the design on the fabric.

Friskit, Maskoid, Liquid Mask   Trade names for a thick gray liquid that is applied to areas of designs to mask them off. A colored ground can then be painted on top of the design, and when the mask is peeled off, the areas underneath will be unaffected.

Georgian or Tweed Weave Paper   An off-white paper with a slightly textured surface.

Gingham   A fabric woven with various plaid, block, or check effects.

Gouache A water-based paint, made with a preparation of gum, that produces a flat, dull, opaque finish.

Gray, Grey, Greige Goods Fabric in a raw, unbleached state, before it is dyed or printed.

Ground Brush A wide brush (usually about 1 to 4 inches) with which to paint colored grounds.

Heat Transfer Printing The technique of printing fabric by transferring a design from special preprinted paper to fabric by heat and pressure. This method can be used only on synthetic fabrics.

Home-Furnishing Designs A general term for fabric designs created for use in the home or for interior decoration.

Knock-Off A design that is inspired by another design, but changed sufficiently to create a new pattern. (Sometimes used pejoratively when a design is merely copied.)

Liberty A blouse-size floral design that gets its name from an English textile company, Liberty of London.

Monochromatic One color used in varying degrees of intensity.

Monotone A design consisting of one color and white.

Motif One figure, element, or unit in a design.

Neutral Coloring A combination of colors, such as beiges, grays, and other muted tones.

Non Crawl, Wax Grip Trade names for a liquid medium that is added to dye or paint to make it adhere to slick-surfaced papers.

Ombre A graduated color effect, ranging from light to dark tones of one color or related colors.

Paisley A design taken from the decorated cashmere shawls of India, adapted and woven in Paisley, Scotland. Paisley is characterized by the palm or curved abstract motif, usually with elaborate detail.

Pastel Coloring A combination of soft, pale colors.

Photographic Printing A method of transferring patterns to fabric by the use of photoengraved rollers.

Piece Goods Printed or plain fabric that is sold by the yard.

Primary Coloring (also called *Bright*) A color combination made up of the primary colors — red, yellow, and blue — and the secondary colors — purple, orange, and green.

Reference Any material that provides inspiration for design ideas. Also, a small painted section of a repeat done to show all the motifs and colors in the design.

Register Mark A mark (usually a cross) that indicates the spot on which to match tracings and drawings so that they are in alignment with each other.

Repeat The technical measurement into which a design must be laid out and painted before it can be printed.

Resist Printing A method of printing in which a substance that resists dyes is used on portions of the fabric. The fabric is then dyed to obtain the wanted color on the untreated portion.

Roller Printing In this process, the design for each color is engraved on a separate copper roller. As the cloth passes through the machine, each roller prints its respective pattern and color on the fabric.

Roman Stripe A series of plain undecorated stripes of varied widths and colors.

Rotary Screen Printing This method utilizes a porous cylinder (one for each color) to hold the design. As dye is forced through a pattern of holes in the cylinder screen, the design is printed on the fabric.

Rubdown A method of transferring a design from tracing paper to drawing paper.

Ruling Pen A mechanical pen that can be filled with ink, paint, or dye for ruling straight lines.

Selvage The reinforced edges on both sides of fabric, which keeps the cloth from unraveling.

Shirting A design with a neat, tailored look, usually a stripe, traditionally used for men's shirts.

Sketch A design before it is put into repeat.

Spatter A technique that uses a toothbrush, paint, and spoon to create a spray of color resembling an airbrush effect.

Squeegee A device used in screen or stencil printing to spread and force the color through the screen or stencil.

Stipple A technique using small dots instead of lines or solid areas for shading.

Strike-Off The first yardage of a pattern printed at the mill, used to check and make changes or corrections.

Stylist The person who directs a design studio and selects the designs and colors to be printed, known as "styling the line."

Stylized   Designs or motifs that are abstracted to varying degrees.

Swatch   A small sample of fabric.

Tempera   An opaque water-based paint, made with an egg preparation, that produces a dull flat finish.

Ticking   A striped cotton cloth used for mattresses and pillow covers.

Toile or Toile de Jouy   A design composed of fine-line pictorial or scenic motifs and used for decorative fabric. Toile de jouy means "cloth from Jouy," Jouy being the French town where these prints originated.

Transfer Paper   A type of carbon paper used to transfer designs from tracing paper to drawing paper.

Warp   The threads that run lengthwise or vertically on a woven fabric.

Waxed Rice Paper   Rice paper that is coated with wax to make it transparent.

Weft or Filling   The crosswise or horizontal threads on a woven fabric.

Bibliography

Books

DESIGN SOURCES

BEER, ALICE BALDWIN. *Trade Goods*. Washington, D.C.: Smithsonian Institution Press, 1970.

BENIDICTUS. *Art Deco Designs in Color*. New York: Dover Publications, Inc., 1979.

BLAKEMORE, FRANCES. *Japanese Design Through Textile Patterns*. New York: John Weatherhill, Inc., 1978.

BOSSERT, HELMUTH TH. *Folk Art of Asia, Africa and The Americas*. New York: Hastings House, 1975.

_____. *Folk Art of Europe*. New York: Hastings House, 1975.

_____. *Peasant Art*. New York: Hastings House, 1975.

D'AVENNES, PRISSE. *Arabic Art In Color*. New York: Dover Publications, Inc., 1978.

EILAND, MURRAY L. *Chinese Exotic Rugs*. New York Graphic Society: Little, Brown and Co., 1979.

FRY, CHARLES RAHN. *Art Deco Designs in Color*. New York: Dover Publications, Inc., 1975.

Full-Color Designs from Chinese Opera Costumes. Edited by The North East Drama Institute, People's Republic of China. New York: Dover Publications, Inc., 1980.

GENTLES, MARGARET. *Turkish and Greek Island Embroideries.* The Art Institute of Chicago, 1964.

GERSPACH, M. *Coptic Textile Designs.* New York: Dover Publications, Inc., 1975.

GITTINGER, MATTIEBELLE. *Splendid Symbols: Textiles and Tradition in Indonesia.* Washington, D.C.: The Textile Museum, 1978.

Heibonsha Survey of Japanese Art, Japanese Costume and Textile Arts. New York: Weatherhill Publications Inc., 1964.

HOLSTEIN, JONATHAN. *The Pieced Quilt, An American Design Tradition.* Greenwich, Conn.: New York Graphic Society Ltd., 1973

HORNER, MARIANNA MERRITT. *The Story of Samplers.* Philadelphia: Philadelphia Museum of Art, 1971.

KING, RONALD. *Botannical Illustration.* New York: Clarkson N. Potter, Inc., 1978.

LEWIS, ALBERT BUELL. *Decorative Art of New Guinea.* New York: Dover Publications, Inc., 1973.

LUBELL, CECIL. *Textile Collections of the World.* Vol. 1, *United States and Canada.* New York: Van Nostrand Reinhold Co., 1976.

———. *Textile Collections of the World.* Vol. 2, *United Kingdom and Ireland.* New York: Van Nostrand Reinhold Co., 1976.

———. *Textile Collections of the World.* Vol. 3, *France.* New York: Van Nostrand Reinhold Co., 1976.

MACKIE, LOUISE W., and ANN P. ROWE. *Masterpieces in the Textile Museum.* Washington, D.C.: The Textile Museum, 1976.

MAILEY, JEAN. *Chinese Silk Tapestry: Ko-ssu.* New York: China Institute in America, 1979.

MENTEN, THEODORE. *Japanese Border Designs.* New York: Dover Publications, Inc., 1977.

MIROW, GREGORY. *A Treasury of Designs for Artists and Craftsmen.* New York: Dover Publications, Inc., 1969.

OSUMI, TAMEZO. *Printed Cottons of Asia.* Published jointly by Bijutsu Shuppan-sha, Tokyo, and Charles E. Tuttle Co., Rutland, Vt., 1963.

PARKER, ANN, and AVON NEAL. *Molas, Folk Art of the Cuna Indians.* Barre, Mass.: Barre Publishing, 1977.

PETTIT, FLORENCE H. *America's Indigo Blues.* New York: Hastings House, 1974.

PLATH, IONA. *The Decorative Arts of Sweden.* New York: Dover Publications, Inc., 1966.

RACINET, A. C. *Handbook of Ornaments in Color.* Four volumes. New York: Van Nostrand Reinhold Co., 1978.

ROSSBACH, ED. *The Art of Paisley.* New York: Van Nostrand Reinhold Co., 1980.

SANO, TAKAHIKO, ed. *Chefs-D'Oeuvre du Musee de L'Impression sur Etoffes, Mulhouse*. Vol. 1, *France I — Alsace and Other French Regions*; Vol. 2, *France II — Jouy, Nantes, Europe and Asia*; Vol. 3, *Printing Designs*. Tokyo: Gakken Co. Ltd., 1979.

SARRE, FRIEDRICH, and HERMAN TRENKWALD. *Oriental Carpet Designs in Full Color*. New York: Dover Publications, Inc., 1979.

SEGUY, E. A. *Exotic Floral Patterns in Color*. New York: Dover Publications, Inc., 1974.

_____. *Full-Color Floral Designs in the Art Nouveau Style*. New York: Dover Publications, Inc., 1977.

_____. *Seguy's Decorative Butterflies and Insects in Full Color*. New York: Dover Publications, Inc., 1977.

SEIBER, ROY. *African Textiles and Decorative Arts*. New York: Museum of Modern Art, 1972.

SMITHSONIAN INSTITUTION. *Kata-Gami: Japanese Stencils in the Collection of the Cooper-Hewitt Museum*. Washington, D.C.: Smithsonian Institution's National Museum of Design, 1979.

STAFFORD, CARLETON L., and ROBERT BISHOP. *America's Quilts and Coverlets*. New York: E. P. Dutton & Co., Inc., 1972.

TUER, ANDREW W. *Japanese Stencil Designs*. New York: Dover Publications, Inc., 1967.

VERNEUIL, M. P. *Art Nouveau Ornament in Color*. New York: Dover Publications, Inc., 1979.

WILKINSON, CHAS. K. *Egyptian Wall Paintings: The MMA Collection of Facsimiles*. New York: Metropolitan Museum of Art, 1979.

WILSON, ERICA. *Crewel Embroidery*. New York: Charles Scribners Sons, 1962.

PRINTING AND HISTORY

DAY, LEWIS F. *Pattern Design*. New York: Dover Publications, Inc., 1979.

LINTON, GEORGE E. *Applied Textiles*. New York: Duell Sloan and Pearce, 1965.

PETTIT, FLORENCE H. *America's Printed and Painted Fabrics*. New York: Hastings House, 1970.

ROBINSON, STUART. *A History of Printed Textiles*. Cambridge, Mass.: The M.I.T. Press, 1969.

Many bookstores and museum shops specialize in material on art and design. One good source for textile designers is Museum Books, Inc., 48 East 43d St., New York, N.Y. 10017.

Magazines

American Fabrics and Fashion. Doric Publishing Corp., New York.
Architectural Digest. Knapp Communications Corp., Los Angeles.
Designers West. Arts Alliance Corp., Los Angeles.

Harper's Bazaar. The Hearst Corp., New York.
House Beautiful. The Hearst Corp., New York.
House and Garden. The Conde Nast Publications, Inc., New York.
Vogue. The Conde Nast Publications, Inc., New York.

The following foreign magazines are available:
Bazaar Italia, Paris Bazaar, Gran Bazaar, Casa Vogue, Paris Vogue, and Elegance.

Newspapers

HFD-Retailing Home Furnishings. New York: Fairchild Publications.
Women's Wear Daily. Fairchild Publications, 7 East 12th Street, New York, N.Y. 10003.

Textile Collections

The Art Institute of Chicago, Michigan Avenue at Adams Street, Chicago, Ill. 60603.

The Brooklyn Museum, Eastern Parkway, Brooklyn, N.Y. 11238.

Cooper-Hewitt Museum of Design, 5th Avenue at 91st Street, New York, N.Y. 10028.

Costume and Textile Study Center, University of Washington, Seattle, Wash. 98195.

Fashion Institute of Technology, Design Laboratory, 27th Street and 7th Avenue, New York, N.Y. 10001.

Los Angeles County Museum of Art, 5905 Wilshire Boulevard, Los Angeles, Cal. 90038.

The Metropolitan Museum of Art, 5th Avenue and 82nd Street, New York, N.Y. 10028.

Museum of Fine Arts, 465 Huntington Avenue, Boston, Mass. 02115.

Museum of the American Indian, Broadway at 155th Street, New York, New York 10032.

Philadelphia Museum of Art, Parkway at 26th Street, Philadelphia, Pa. 19101.

The Textile Museum, 2320 S. Street N.W., Washington, D.C. 20008.

Crafts Sources

American Craft. American Craft Council, New York. Bi-monthly magazine.

The Crafts Report, 700 Orange Street, P.O. Box 1992, Wilmington, Del. 19899. Newsletter; covers finances, health hazards, supplies, fairs, and tax information.

Craftworkers Market. Writer's Digest Books, 9933 Alliance Road, Cincinnati, Ohio 45242. Issued yearly; complete directory of markets, suppliers, courses, agents.

Professional Organization

Textile Designers Guild, 30 East 20th Street, Room 405, New York, N.Y. 10003. Information; 212-982-9298.

Index

Layout, repeat, 72. *See also*
  Repeat
Liberty design, 31. *See also*
  Designing
Light box, 94
Line-up, 52
Liquid mask, 19. *See also*
  Masking technique
Liquid soap, 18, 92. *See also*
  Non Crawl
Luma concentrated watercolor,
  11

M

Madder design, *see* Foulard
  design
Magic marker, *see* Marking
  pen, felt-tip
Man-made fabrics, 114
Marking pen, felt-tip, 17, 94, 98,
  103
Masa waxed rice paper, *see*
  Rice paper, waxed
Masking tape, 101
Masking technique, 19
Maskoid, 19
Materials, *see* Brushes; Paints;
  Paper
Men's wear, *see* Apparel
  designs
Mi-Teinte, *see* Paper, colored
Mill work, 116
Monotone design, 29-30. *See
  also* Designing
Mounting, 6

N

Non Crawl, 11, 18, 92, 93

O

One-way layout, 35, 50, 51, 87
Originality, design, 21, 22, 27

P

Packed layout, *see* All-over
  layout
Paints, 9-12

Paints, opaque, *see* Gouache;
  Tempera
Paisley design, 44-45, 74. *See
  also* Designing
Palette, 16
Paper, 12-13
Paper, colored, 13. *See also*
  Grounds, colored
Paper, opaque, 63, 84, 94
Patchwork design, 30-31, 61.
  See also Designing
Patchwork layout, 60. *See also*
  Patchwork design
Patterns, *see* Designs
Peasant design, *see* Folk
  design
Pen, dotting, 98, *see* Stipple
  technique
Pen, Pilot (Sc-uf), 15
Pen, ruling, 19-20, 35, 41, 55,
  57
Pen, technical drawing, 15, 98
Pen point, Crow Quill, 15-16
Pen point, Joseph Gillot, 15
Pencil, colored, 38, *see* Stipple
  technique
Pencil sharpener, 17
Pencil, tracing, 17
Portfolio, 6-7
Printing process, 71-72, 108-16
Pro-white, 18
Provincial design, *see* Folk
  design

R

Razor blade, single-edge, 15,
  107
Record book, 5, *see* Studio,
  design
Reference material, sources of,
  23-25, 28-29
Repeats, 2, 3, 4, 7, 71-89
Rice paper, waxed, 6, 11, 12,
  16, 18, 49, 63, 70, 85, 86,
  92-93, 94, 95, 107
Rich Art Tempera, 10
Roller, paint, 67, *see* Grounds,
  colored
Roller printing, 63, 71, 72, 73,
  108-10. *See also* Screen
  printing; Printing process
Rotary screen printing, 110-11.
  See also printing process

V

Vertical repeat, 73, 74, 76-80, 83. *See also* Half-drop repeat; Square repeat

W

Wallpaper, *see* Home furnishing designs
Warp design, 43-44. *See also* Designing

Warp technique, 102-3
Watercolors, concentrated, *see* Dyes, transparent
Wax grip, *see* Non Crawl
Waxed rice paper, *see* Rice paper
 brushes, 13
 Designers Gouache, 10
Women's wear, *see* Apparel designs
Women's Wear Daily, 23